PRINT FORMATS AND FINISHES

A RotoVision Book

Published and distributed by RotoVision
Route Suisse 9
CH-1295 Mies
Switzerland

RotoVision SA
Sales and Editorial Office
Sheridan House, 114 Western Road
Hove BN3 1DD, UK

Tel: +44 (0)1273 72 72 68
Fax: +44 (0)1273 72 72 69
www.rotovision.com

10 9 8 7 6 5 4 3 2 1

ISBN: 978-2-88893-136-2

Art Director Tony Seddon
Design by Studio Ink
This edition compiled and edited by Diane Leyman

Printing and binding in China by
1010 Printing International Ltd

PRINT FORMATS AND FINISHES

The Designer's Illustrated Guide to Brochures, Catalogs, Bags, Labels, Packaging, and Promotion

Edward Denison, Roger Fawcett-Tang, Jessica Glaser, Carolyn Knight, Loewy, and Scott Witham

RotoVision

CONTENTS

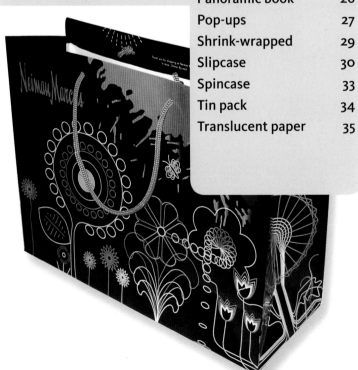

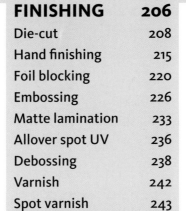

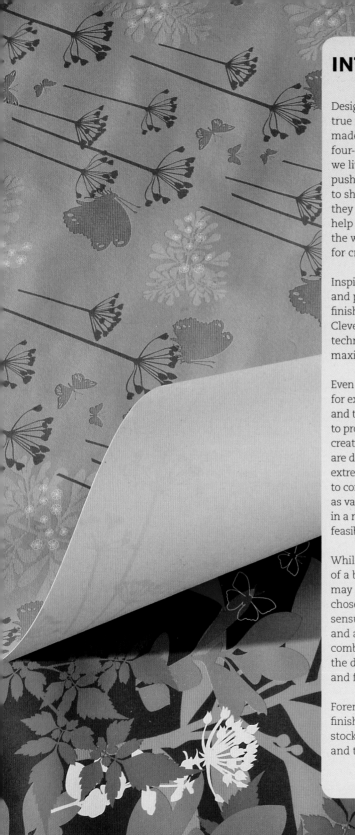

INTRODUCTION

Designing for print is easy. That would be true if the world lacked imagination, if designers made no effort, and printers took on only simple four-color work. Thankfully, this isn't the world we live in. Even on limited budgets, designers push at every opportunity, manufacturers strive to show off what they can do with the machinery they have, and clients want only the very best to help them stand out from the crowd. This makes the world a far more exciting and testing place for creatives designing for print.

Inspirational design is made real through print and production processes. Good printing and finishing will make a great job even better. Clever use of formats, materials, and unusual techniques will ensure that the work gains maximum exposure and praise.

Even on a limited budget there is always room for experimentation. Advances in technology and transglobal production have allowed designers to produce cost-effective solutions, as well as being creatively ambitious and adventurous. No longer are designers restricted by printing presses with extremely limited operations; it is now possible to combine full color with other options such as varnish, fluorescents, and metallic inks, in a manner that was not economically feasible a few years ago.

While the physical and visual characteristics of a brochure, package, or promotional item may perform a necessary practical role, the chosen finish can provide visual, tactile, and sensuous qualities that can excite, intrigue, and assist the user. Commercially, the effective combination of these processes can even mean the difference between spectacular success and failure.

Foremost in influencing the choice of printing finish is the material itself. The range of paper stock available to designers today is bewildering, and the different coatings, lamination, board types, and weights will impact significantly on the final appearance of the job. Equally, using metal, plastic, glass, or other less common materials requires special attention when considering printing options.

While different effects can be achieved on different materials, the type of manufacturing process presents even more choice for designers. Depending on the type of material, all manner of different finishes can be achieved by processes such as embossing, debossing, die-cutting, stamping, molding, and etching. These production processes can be applied to the material in a way that alters the entire surface texture or enhances specific details, but it is when they are used together with printing that the full extent of finishing opportunities available to designers is truly realized.

The combination of printing and production finishes offers virtually no limit to the range and extent of finishes that can be achieved, but designers should remain vigilant to the environmental cost of this choice. Printing and production finishes are at times misconstrued as being superfluous, since their role is often directed at adding value rather than meaning. In an age where environmentally conscious design is not simply experiencing a resurgence but its future role is imperative, the designer's choice of printing and production techniques should always consider the environmental impact of a design.

The selection of case studies presented in this book aims to showcase a wide range of finishes used in different scenarios from across the industry, including brochures, catalogs, bags, labels, packaging, and promotion. The selection draws from an international array of examples that either employ printing finishes, production finishes, or both—from the common to the unique, from the simple to the complex, and from the cost-effective to the lavish. It is a celebration of all that is special in print and production finishes, and hopefully goes a long way to inspire, inform, and motivate designers, thereby helping to stimulate future design projects.

FORMATS

TOPSHOP MEMBERSHIP CARD

DESIGN	CLIENT
DESIGN N/A	**TOPSHOP**

SPECIFICATIONS
- ➔ Screen printed mirror
- ➔ Polythene bag
- ➔ White leather pouch
- ➔ Gloss white box
- ➔ Rub-down lettering

010

M250 is a membership card that takes the form of a mirror. It is sent out by British clothing retailer Topshop to 250 leading fashion editors, stylists, and celebrities, entitling them to a personalized shopping service. Each year the style of mirror is changed, and has ranged from antique to smoked to bronze. It is cut, beveled, and polished from 6mm (c. ¼in) glass. For this membership pack, the square gray mirror was screen printed on both sides, then vacuum sealed within a large square polythene bag, also screen printed, with 250 dots. The bag was then packed in a white leather, hole-punched pouch, in a cube-shaped, gloss white box. Each box was addressed by hand with luminous rub-down lettering.

DURAN DURAN CD BOX SET

DESIGN
KUKUSI

CLIENT
DURAN DURAN / THEMUSIC.COM

SPECIFICATIONS
➔ Flip-top box
➔ Gatefold cardboard sleeves
➔ Fifth color silver
➔ Hand-stamped typography

These gatefold CDs were recorded during Duran Duran's live gigs, then sold immediately afterward. The city and date were hand-stamped after the recording and prior to sale, adding an element of authenticity and providing an endorsed way to create and distribute "bootleg" recordings. Fans could build their set according to the gigs they attended. The floral designs are based on Japanese woodcuts, referencing the Japanese leg of the tour.

011

The flip-top box format allowed fans to collect all seven live recordings, sold separately, and build their own box set in the process—a new spin on the term "collector's edition."

THE BEST OF R.E.M. BOX SET

DESIGN
CHRONICTOWN

CLIENT
WARNER BROS/WEA

SPECIFICATIONS
- ➜ Matte finish
- ➜ Double-lid, wrapped cardboard box
- ➜ 18 CD sleeves

A "best of" box set, the packaging for this singles collection is based on old 45 record boxes. For this promotional item, with a limited run of 3,000, the agency used the slightly different format and matte finish to make the box feel special. The agency also felt that, with the dense card weight, the matte finish would give the packaging a touch of quality and tactility. One of the biggest challenges was the fact that, as some of the singles are almost 20 years old, the original cover artwork had been created before the era of digital design, which meant that some of the artwork had to be recreated from the original source material.

This compact packaging is a great way of housing a singles collection, without resorting to putting the tracks onto a single compilation CD. The double flip-top harks back to old record boxes and gives the packaging extra sturdiness and longevity.

014

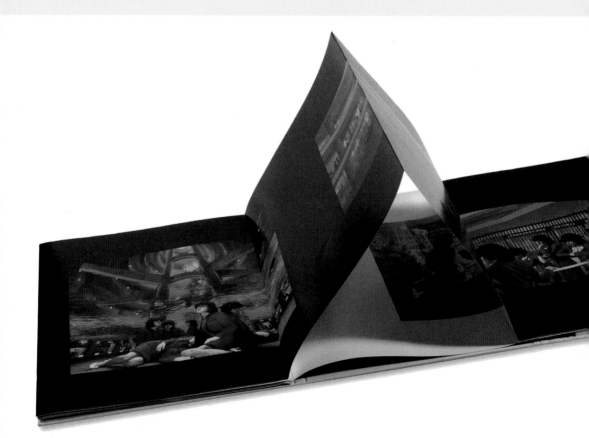

MIWA YANAGI MONOGRAPH

DESIGN
SURFACE/SIWA YANAGI

CLIENT
MIWA YANAGI

SPECIFICATIONS
- 44 pages plus 78 pages printed four-color process and black only
- Concertina-folded
- Perfect-bound

This monograph for the Japanese artist Miwa Yanagi incorporates two very different elements. Within the six-page, gatefold cover is a concertina-folded color section on the left, and on the right, a monochromatic textbook with small, black-and-white reproductions of the work, together with a series of essays and interviews.

The concertina section is unusual in the way the images and text are positioned; both image and text wrap around the folded pages, encouraging the reader to unfold and extend the spreads. The front of the concertina section shows one series of images set on a white background, and the reverse shows another series set on black.

Two very different books are housed within the same cover; the three-panel cover allows for two spines. The left book extends as a long, concertina-folded section, while the right book is more conventionally bound.

015

REMOTE CD PACKAGING

DESIGN	CLIENT
ZIP DESIGN	**TUNDRA RECORDS**

SPECIFICATIONS
- Jewel case
- Foldout poster insert on uncoated, recycled stock

This packaging uses a simple foldout poster on recycled matte stock as an insert. Colors and type are kept to an absolute minimum so as not to compete with the illustrations by Lance Sells, which were inspired by Arctic flowers and isolation.

The recycled stock lends itself well to this packaging, which is also reflected in the unusual matte finish of the CD itself. It's also refreshing to see packaging that respects the illustrations, rather than overcrowding them with print.

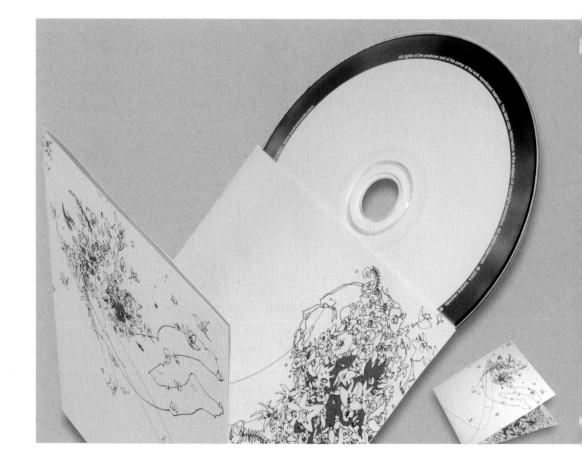

By printing large-format posters (841 × 1,189mm/33 × 46^3/$_4$in) and cutting the excess posters down to A4 (210 × 297mm/8^1/$_8$ × 11^5/$_8$in), Mode were able to create a range of A4 letterheads that the client could overprint as and when required—a great way to get maximum value from print.

FORMATS // LARGE-FORMAT POSTERS

LEE MAWDSLY POSTERS

DESIGN	CLIENT
MODE	**LEE MAWDSLY**

SPECIFICATIONS
➔ A0-sized posters
➔ Four-color printing with single metallic special
➔ 60gsm Tercoat Plus stock

Lee Mawdsly approached Mode to help increase his profile within the creative industry. Mode's approach let the quality of the images speak for themselves. A series of large A0 (841 × 1,189mm/33 × 46¾in) format posters was printed by The Ordnance Survey—the only company with a printing press large enough.

Lee's stationery range was formed by chopping up his posters at the time of production. This not only produced a very striking and memorable identity, but also saved significantly on production costs. The entire job was printed on 60gsm Tercoat Plus by Tervakoski using a four-color process with a single metallic special to create 800 posters, 50 of which were trimmed to create 800 letterheads.

BONOBO CD DESIGN

DESIGN
RED DESIGN

CLIENT
BONOBO/NINJA TUNE

SPECIFICATIONS
- ◗ Gatefold CD wallet with 12-page booklet and inner CD sleeve
- ◗ Case: heavy board with matte-laminate finish
- ◗ Booklet: silk stock, UV finish
- ◗ CD Sleeve: matte UV

Wanting to capture the filmic quality of Bonobo's music, Red Design took a series of abstract and figurative images. Both organic and intriguing, they resemble stills from a film. Unfortunately, there was no budget for imagery, so the agency resorted to raiding its own personal collections, as well as the work of its late friend, Dominic Howard.

However, Red Design was pretty happy with the outcome, as the "images seem more personal and scrapbook-like." The photos' subject matter and colors give the piece something of a retro feel, which is further reflected in the format. Using a slightly discolored heavy board gatefold wallet, the agency has created packaging reminiscent of the vinyl album covers from the late 1960s and early 1970s.

019

This gatefold CD packaging neatly holds the material in place. The use of heavy board harks back to the era of vinyl albums.

PURE IDEAS NOKIA BROCHURE

DESIGN
NOKIA DESIGN BRAND TEAM

CLIENT
NOKIA

SPECIFICATIONS
- 92 pages plus 48 small-format pages
- Four-page cover and dust jacket printed one color and four-color process plus various specials and varnishes
- Perfect-bound

Produced as an internal document for Nokia, this brochure visually catalogs the research and development of the Nokia Design Brand Team. A minimal white cover conceals the lavishly produced contents held within. The cover has the title foil blocked in a clear varnish, with the Nokia logo printed in blue at the foot; and a dust jacket wraps around the cover, which unfolds into a large poster. Inside, the brand's corporate colors of white, blue, and green are introduced by a single sheet of an uncoated green stock. This is followed by a 16-page section on a pale blue uncoated stock printed in the corporate blue, and this section contains an interview with three key members of the design team. The brochure then switches to a coated silk stock as it visually illustrates the corporate colors, typography, photographic treatments, and graphic treatments, and finally ends with a series of images from the design studio. Throughout the brochure are a series of small pages printed on a light weight of cast-coated stock (gloss on one side and matte on the reverse). The brochure makes extensive use of a spot machine varnish and a color-tinted machine varnish to highlight areas of the page, echoing the size and position of the small inset pages or used as borders for full-bleed images, and so on.

A series of inset pages appear throughout the brochure, always trimmed flush to the base of the book. These pages are used to provide additional information on the design principles. Even on pages without this inset page, the same area is often highlighted in a UV varnish.

THE PRODUCTION KITCHEN PROMOTIONAL MATERIAL

DESIGN
BLOK DESIGN

CLIENT
THE PRODUCTION KITCHEN

SPECIFICATIONS
➔ Flexible brochure with interchanging parts,
   printed on various stock

The Production Kitchen is dedicated to producing and printing creative projects for the design and advertising industry. For this project, spare graphics and complex linear patterns were combined to express both the nature of the business and the passion the company has for the print production process itself. There is a certain playfulness in the graphics and slanted text that appears and disappears consistently depending on the application. Blok's choice of materials influenced the experimental aspect of print design: they created a flexible brochure in which parts can be interchanged and updated without having to reprint the entire project.

021

ARTEK INVITATION

DESIGN
EMMI SALONEN

CLIENT
ARTEK

SPECIFICATIONS
➲ Munken Polar, FSC-certified paper

The product launch of a new range of bamboo furniture from a renowned Swedish manufacturer was inevitably also an opportunity to celebrate the environmental and ecological benefits of this remarkable material. Invitations for the launch introduced to potential consumers the unique qualities and environmental benefits that bamboo possesses, and the ways in which it can reflect their lifestyle choices.

The design of the leaflet, A5-sized (148 × 210mm/5¾ × 8¼in), yet manufactured from a single piece of folded A3 (297 × 240mm/11¾ × 16½in) paper, reflects these qualities. The clean horizontal lines on the front and back cover echo the grain of the bamboo, which is partially revealed in print on the inner surface of the invitation. Design, rather than materials and printing, was the key tool through which environmental benefits were achieved in this work. The deliberate use of standard-sized papers reduced setup times and also costs, and minimized waste material.

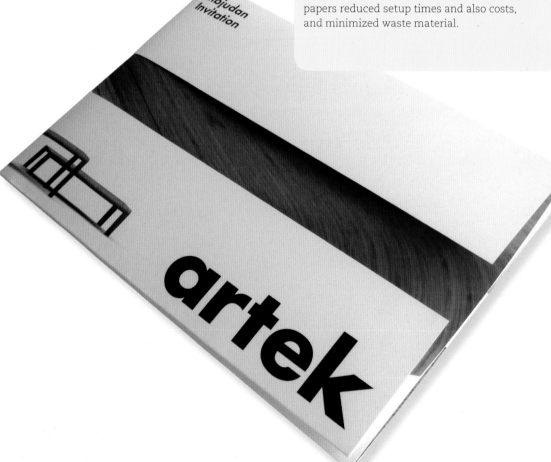

A single piece of A5 paper was used as an insert that contained more detailed information about the event and allowed personalized invitations to be made efficiently and without additional environmentally and financially costly processes.

Inbjudan
Invitation

Ekologisk brunch hos Artek
Organic brunch at Artek

artek

Precision-molded polystyrene foam was created by California-based Tempo Foam from artwork supplied by Turnstyle. Molded and cast foam allows for fine detail in the finishing, in addition to being incredibly tough and durable.

TEAGUE PORTFOLIO MAILER

DESIGN	CLIENT
TURNSTYLE	**TEAGUE**

SPECIFICATIONS
- Domtar Luna Matte
- Polystyrene box
- CMYK with a single spot color
- Aqueous coating

The limited-edition (totalling 325) Teague portfolio mailer was intended to create awareness for Teague's unique design perspective as evident through its body of work. Teague has been around for 80+ years and is well known in the industrial design sector as a legacy company, but less well known for its more recent innovative work. The mailer aimed to communicate how Teague's 80 years of experience help to inform its work today.

This bespoke mailer was created with Domtar Luna Matte and a custom-made polystyrene box. It used conventional CMYK printing with a single spot color and was finished with an overall aqueous coating.

025

RENAISSANCE BOOK

DESIGN	CLIENT
THE KITCHEN	**RENAISSANCE**

SPECIFICATIONS
- ➔ 36 pages plus casebound cover
- ➔ Four-color process plus UV and machine varnishes
- ➔ Sewn-through sections

To accompany the tenth anniversary of the nightclub/record label Renaissance, The Kitchen avoided CD packaging methods and opted for an extremely long, thin, panoramic-format book. The format is derived from the placement of three CDs end-to-end on the inside back cover. Elaborate full-color illustrations formed from fragments of previously released CDs are given greater depth by floral elements, which are printed using a "dirty" varnish. The book is broken into different sections, each of which is divided by a sheet of thick, white simulator paper with the title printed on it in black and gold type. The book is thread-sewn "sewn through"—a binding method achieved by sewing from front to back, forming a very strong bind.

This book uses white simulator paper with the text printed in black and gold. Machine and spot UV varnishes are employed to add greater depth to the illustrations.

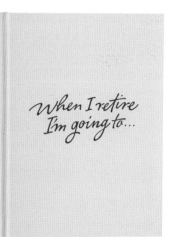

When I retire I'm going to...

MAP FINANCIAL SERVICES BROCHURE

DESIGN	CLIENT
VOICE	**MAP FINANCIAL SERVICES**

SPECIFICATIONS
- ➔ White pop-up book
- ➔ Printed in one color

MAP Financial Services asked Voice to design a standard A4 (210 × 297mm/8¼ × 11¾in) brochure to promote its financial planning business. However, Voice soon discovered that MAP actually needed a unique item to make it more memorable with potential customers.

As MAP develops financial solutions that are specifically dictated by its customers' lifestyle choices, the design used the pop-up book medium coupled with simple rhyming verses to stimulate imagination and encourage memorability through interactivity. The book was produced all in white to give the viewer free rein to take this story and make it their own.

027

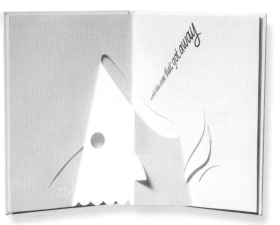

wish like one that got away

Pop-ups can be created by die-cutting pages, but, instead of fully removing the die-cut section, adding scoring and folding against the natural direction of the folded pages. When the page is opened, the pop-up will leap out.

Feel like a million dollars every day...

A thick, white, dotted line is printed on the three sides of the booklet that require trimming. With these edges trimmed off, the book becomes usable in a conventional manner.

CIVIC TRUST AWARDS BOOKLET

DESIGN
SANS+BAUM

CLIENT
CIVIC TRUST AWARDS

SPECIFICATIONS
- 40 pages, self-cover
- Printed in five specials
- Saddle-stitched

This very small booklet, produced to celebrate the 40th anniversary of the Civic Trust Awards in the United Kingdom, is contained in shrink-wrapped plastic. Once the plastic has been removed, it becomes apparent that the booklet requires some interaction in order for its contents to be read. Formed from a single sheet of paper, the booklet has been folded and saddle-stitched, but the folded edges have not been trimmed down. The user must finish this process in order to read the material. The cover includes instructions on how to "remove wrapping, cut along dotted line, read pages from left to right." The booklet is printed in three different specials on either side of the sheet; green, turquoise, and black on one side and orange, purple, and black on the other. Due to the nature of the folded sheet, some spreads are in three colors and others in five.

029

The broadsheet and 35mm transparencies are housed within a toploading slipcase. The transparency sheet is formed by bonding two sheets of grayboard together. The top sheet features a series of die-cut holes of the exact shape and size required to hold the transparencies.

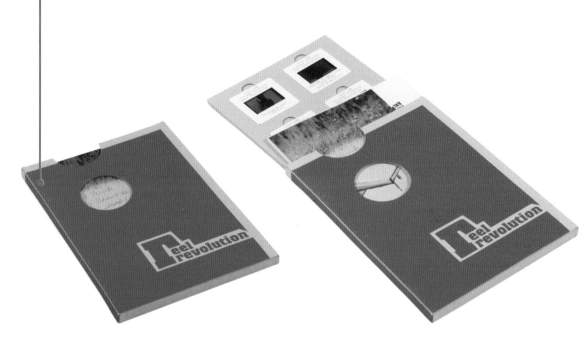

LEVI'S VINTAGE CLOTHING BOOK

DESIGN
OLIVER WALKER

CLIENT
LEVI'S

SPECIFICATIONS

- ➔ 16-panel folded sheet plus slipcase
- ➔ Four-color printing process
- ➔ Cover screen printed in one color
- ➔ Embossed

Housed inside a custom-made, grayboard slipcase, this book for Levi's Vintage Clothing has a very loose graphic style. The slipcase is screen printed in a single color, with the title printed and embossed to add a tactile dimension to the piece. A circular, die-cut hole reveals some hand-written text on the folded brochure within. Inside are two more sheets of the same grayboard with recesses cut to hold a series of 35mm slides. Not only do these show the fashion collection off to good effect, but also, as the pack is sent out to fashion journalists, they can be used for reproduction in magazines. Also included is a 16-panel, folded brochure with cut-up images from the collection montaged with scribbled comments and doodles. One of the panels has another sheet of grayboard affixed, with a die-cut circle used to hold a CD in place.

This fluorescent spincase packaging is unusual, creating immediate standout. However, the color and format are clearly very dominant, so it's important that the CD within is designed with this in mind.

LOEWY CD PACKAGE
DESIGN: LOEWY

DESIGN/CLIENT
LOEWY

SPECIFICATIONS
➔ Fluorescent polypropylene spincase
➔ One-color print onto matte white CD

With the self-imposed financial constraints on this project, Loewy decided to print in just one color. The stringent budget focused the design, which was kept simple, rather than overelaborated. The agency believes that "what you leave out is as important as what you leave in." In this instance, the matte white background allows the hard black contemporary typography to leap out. The design is then brought alive by the fluorescent orange spincase.

GAME LAUNCH PRESS PACK

DESIGN
999 DESIGN

CLIENT
SONY PLAYSTATION 2

SPECIFICATIONS
- CD
- Wire-o bound instruction manual
- Mock Polaroid pictures
- Human hair
- Foam-lined metal tin
- Brown paper
- Tape outer wrapping

Designed to promote the launch of The Getaway for the PlayStation 2 in the UK and Europe, 999 Design wanted to create a press pack ransom-note package with an authentic look and feel—mirroring the theme of the game itself. Sent to games journalists wrapped in brown paper, the tin pack resembles a foam-lined gun case and contains a doctored A to Z instruction manual, Polaroid stills from the game, a sample of human hair, as well as a press disc of the game itself. And the greatest challenge the agency faced? Getting permission to use UK Ordnance Survey maps—and real human hair.

There are lots of elements at play in this pack that combine to produce a piece with real standout. It's clearly a very polished end product, but touches such as the brown-paper-and-tape wrapping, and scrawled marker handwriting make it feel more authentic.

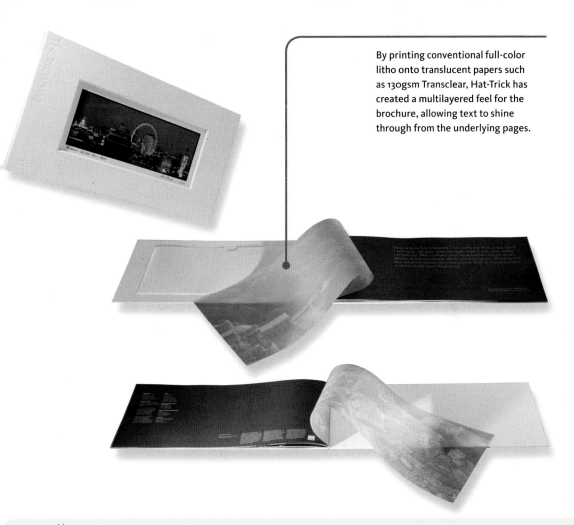

By printing conventional full-color litho onto translucent papers such as 130gsm Transclear, Hat-Trick has created a multilayered feel for the brochure, allowing text to shine through from the underlying pages.

LAND SECURITIES BROCHURE

DESIGN
HAT-TRICK DESIGN

CLIENT
LAND SECURITIES

SPECIFICATIONS
- Robert Horne, GF Smith, and Tullis Russell papers
- Debossing with spot clear foil blocking

035

Land Securities needed a promotional sales brochure for its luxury penthouse The View in London. The front cover showed the property's fantastic views over London—a photograph was taken from the penthouse overlooking London and was framed as a limited-edition print.

The brochure is a stunning piece of promotional literature. It is printed on Robert Horne, GF Smith, and Tullis Russell papers (text: 170gsm Parilux Matt; intro sheet: 130gsm Transclear; covers: 350gsm Duplexed Colorplan Pristine White, 1,750 micron Duplex t; endpapers: 250gsm Invercote). The cover text is debossed with a spot clear foil blocking.

MATERIALS

A single-sided, single-color image of cornflowers is held inside a narrower, folded tag, and tied with rustic string to the Spa Bath Salts bag. All layers of the hangtag are printed on textured white card and, together with the attached wooden scoop, enhance the classic country style of this item.

BATH HOUSE NATURAL SPA RANGE

DESIGN/CLIENT
BATH HOUSE

SPECIFICATIONS
- Single- and two-color lithography
- Textured paper
- String
- Fabric

By introducing a variety of materials into the range of labels and hangtags for its Natural Spa products, Bath House has been able to print in just two colors—brown and black—to realize extremely stylish, quality packaging that, as the manufacturer suggests, "reflects the wild beauty of the British countryside." On the bottles, very simple circular and rectangular labels are visually enhanced as they integrate with natural string; around the sack of Bath Salts, a single-color round white label is attached to, and complements, a band of light brown, heavyweight, textured paper.

A single-color label for White Meadow soap is held in place by a waxy translucent paper. This not only wraps around the label and the soap, but also creates a visually "misty" effect. A piece of string is tied in a knot on top to complete the traditional styling.

MATERIALS // FABRIC

SPOOK PROMOTIONAL MATERIALS

DESIGN	CLIENT
STANDARD13	**SPOOK**

SPECIFICATIONS
- 300gsm and 170gsm Munken Lynx White stock
- Machine stitching
- Fuse wire
- Cotton scarf

Spook is an independent Melbourne fashion label. These promotional materials were produced to launch its brand and inaugural collection in fall 2003. The general invitation was printed onto a swing tag presented alongside a catalog (both machine stitched). The catalog was hung on a miniature coat hanger that could fold out into a 396 × 228mm (15¾ × 9in) poster. It was designed so that as each section was unfolded, it revealed a new item from the collection, showing the contact details last. VIP guests received their invitation on a machine-stitched cotton scarf. Materials used included cotton, 300gsm and 170gsm Munken Lynx White, and fuse wire. The sewing machine used by Standard13 had no inbuilt memory, so all the sewing had to be done in one session.

ZOLOFOLIO
PRESENTATION CASE

DESIGN/CLIENT
PALAZZOLO DESIGN

SPECIFICATIONS
◗ Cut and stitched carpet padding

Designers are constantly on the lookout for unusual materials that can enrich their work, enhance its individuality, ensure its memorability, and generally make their designs stand out from the crowd. Palazzolo Design sourced a unique material from the totally different context of carpeting. The company was looking to create a special case to hold client presentation samples that would say something about the distinctive personality of the Palazzolo brand.

041

The carpet padding has been cut and stitched along each edge to create an unusual, long-lasting container. The durability of this sturdy textile, along with the individuality of its recycled composition, ensures that each case will be kept longer than many of its paper-based alternatives.

MATERIALS // RIBBON & CLOTHESPIN

BATH HOUSE
BATHING SUGARS

DESIGN/CLIENT
BATH HOUSE

SPECIFICATIONS
- Two- and four-color printing
- Ribbon
- Miniature clothespin

Very attractive and unusual use of materials within the labeling of these Bath House Bathing Sugars converts simple white-paper bags into desirable purchases. Two-color labels on the fronts of the bags pursue a fresh, traditional theme, while the combination of four-color labels, single-color labels, ribbons, and clothespins wrapping around the tops to secure the bags creates an extremely pretty and appealing presentation.

The back view of the top label and fastening mechanism on Shantung Silk reveals an amazing attention to detail: the red, orange, and gold silky ribbon feeds through a slit in the label, folds up and over the bag, and is held in place together with a single-color tag by a delightful little wooden clothespin. The synergy of such an interesting mix of materials, grouped with so much care and consideration, makes these products appear handmade and irresistible.

WUNDERBURG DESIGN ENVELOPES

DESIGN/CLIENT
WUNDERBURG DESIGN

SPECIFICATIONS
- Smoked sealing wax
- Personal seal

"Using carefully selected materials to create harmony and interest is an important component in our corporate design," says Annette Ruland of Wunderburg Design. With this philosophy in mind, Wunderburg seals its gray DL envelopes with smoked gray sealing wax, imprinting it with the company's personal stamp to form a striking and unusual three-dimensional "sticker." This clever use of traditional material in a contemporary color, and on a stylish envelope, immediately communicates to recipients Wunderburg's unique thinking and design expertise.

043

044   BOOKLET IN ZIPLOCK BAG

DESIGN
PAUL HOGARTH + FLAVOUR

CLIENT
ARGONAUT ROWING CLUB, CANADA

SPECIFICATIONS
➔ Waterproof Ziploc bag
➔ Screen printing

In celebration of the 130th anniversary of a renowned rowing club, a small portable logbook was created that members could take with them whenever they rowed, giving them the option to log up to 200 results. The diminutive 64-page booklet was printed in a single color on tinted paper stock with a black cover on which the title was foil stamped above a motif of a rower. The aim of the book was to be both useful and inspirational for current and future club members. The question of how to package this reusable product was therefore a challenging one. Like the booklet itself, the design solution lay in simplicity. In deference to the sport, a waterproof opaque Ziploc bag was used, on the front of which was printed a brief and witty remark in the same typeface used on the cover the booklet. The choice of package, material, and finish, and the overall relationship it has with the product, make this an excellent packaging solution for a very specific brief.

MONTEZUMA'S BAGS

DESIGN/CLIENT
MONTEZUMA'S CHOCOLATES LTD.

SPECIFICATIONS
➔ Flexography
➔ Frosted plastic
➔ Brown paper
➔ Cellophane

045

Montezuma's produces a diverse range of bags made from interesting and contrasting materials, including frosted plastic, brown paper, and cellophane.

The range of bags covers every eventuality and marketing opportunity: frosted plastic bags give customers a tantalizing glimpse of Montezuma's products while also ensuring company branding is paramount; single-color blue is used across all these different surfaces; the visual language of the brown-paper bags emphasizes the handmade, organic nature of the chocolate; and the small cellophane bag, subtly printed with the company's Aztec illustration, ensures that customers making even the smallest purchase will have a branded memento.

BIODEGRADABLE POOP BAGS

DESIGN
MODERN DOG (ILLUSTRATIONS BY VITTORIO COSTARELLA)

CLIENT
OLIVE, GREEN GOODS FOR MODERN DOGS

SPECIFICATIONS
- Biodegradable plastic bags
- Aluminum lid
- Cardboard tube
- 100 percent PCW paper label
- Printed with soy-based inks

Respecting the environment is second nature for most responsible pet owners, and an important part of this role is picking up the mess that pets leave behind. While some local authorities provide waste bins specifically designed for depositing this mess, most situations demand that owners use their own resources. This is often achieved by scooping the mess into a plastic bag, manufactured from non-renewable and non-biodegradable materials, and thrown in a waste bin from where it will be transported to landfill and left to sit until perhaps discovered by bemused archaeologists hundreds of years from now.

However, this inexcusable misuse of resources, second only to the disposable baby diaper when dealing with natural waste, need not be so environmentally detrimental any longer. With the advent of biodegradable plastic, animal waste can be collected and disposed of in a way that will not linger for hundreds of years. The packaging for these biodegradable poop bags has been designed specifically to be eco-friendly, functional, and attractive. The smart untreated and contrasting natural materials of cardboard and aluminum make the package a stylish product, while the label, printed using soy-based inks in a range of soft tones on 100 percent PCW waste paper, provides a cheerful and jocular finish.

50
Poop
Bags
100% Biodegradable
Made with GMO-free corn
Olive
Green Goods for Modern Dogs
Manufactured by BioBag

PRANK FUN PACK

DESIGN/CLIENT
PRANK DESIGN

SPECIFICATIONS
➔ Transparent plastic bag
➔ Two-color screen printing

When creating this Fun Pack, Prank Design wanted to exploit the visual language of children's "goodie bags." To this end the company selected transparent plastic bags to hold a selection of brightly colored card and sticker-based promotional items, and sealed these with a foldover silkscreened label stapled into place. The transparent plastic bag allows the recipient a tantalizing view of the "goodies" contained within.

047

KIRSTY MCLEOD SKINCARE RANGE

DESIGN
PAUL CARTWRIGHT BRANDING

CLIENT
KIRSTY MCLEOD

SPECIFICATIONS
- Fedrigoni cartonboard
- Screen printing
- Blind embossing

This range of off-the-shelf bottles and jars in bespoke cartons was produced for premium skincare specialist Kirsty McLeod. The client's existing identity was a simple two-color logo: an ornate green frame surrounded the name printed in black. In order to create maximum standout and a sophisticated and desirable finished product, a very white, embossed board from Fedrigoni was chosen for the carton material. The logo was then screen printed onto the front, with ingredients and usage printed on the reverse, and a version of the logo blind-embossed on the sides. This created a "chain" effect around the pack and allowed the product to be displayed with alternate print, emboss, print, etc. on the shelf.

Frosted glass jars and bottles maintain a uniformity across the range, and also allow customers a firmer grip when using the product.

COLOMBO OIL PACKAGING

DESIGN	CLIENT
ASA SAN MARINO	**VARIOUS**

SPECIFICATIONS
- ➔ UV-printing
- ➔ Tinplate
- ➔ Cardboard
- ➔ Die-cutting

Different materials used together in primary, secondary, and sometimes tertiary packaging can create a memorable effect that enhances the presentation of the overall package. This approach is frequently used with high-end products, where the added outlay in extra packaging materials can be borne by the relatively high price of the product. However, this need not be confined only to the most exclusive product ranges. Through clever design, different materials, production techniques, and printing can be combined in efficient and highly effective ways. In this example, the packaging for olive oil includes a cartonboard outer container that has been die-cut to accommodate the shaped steel bottle securely. The refreshing design has been effectively applied to both surfaces so that when combined, they blend into one another and appear to be one. This effect is complicated by having to print on the curves of the metal container without distortion, which would become more apparent against the flat surface of the cartonboard outer package.

Different materials reproduce inks in very different ways, so the continuity of the graphic image across cartonboard and metal when both components of the packaging are united requires careful consideration. The die-cut also plays an important role in securing the bottle while in transit as well as at the point of sale, and reinforces the continuity of the pattern by holding the bottle in place.

MATERIALS // CARTONBOARD

HEFTI JEUNESSE ICE CREAM TUBS

DESIGN
HELVETICA

CLIENT
BÖÖGG JAPAN

SPECIFICATIONS
- Coated cartonboard
- Polypropylene film on gloss paper

This range of frozen products from a Swiss chocolatier designed for sale in Japan has had to consider how the distinctive attributes of the product should be portrayed to a receptive market, but one in which the ingredients and flavors used might be unfamiliar. The coated cartonboard container has been given a printing treatment that is eminently attractive in its own right, but equally and classically geared to Japanese taste through the use of pale colors and measured graphic patterns. Soft tones printed in a single color—different for each flavor—on a white background produce a finish that distinguishes each product type while retaining a unity across the entire range. Foremost in establishing this sense of brand cohesion is the application on each design of a band of printed gold with a textured silky finish, suggestive of brushed metal, around the rim of the lid, which affirms the brand's distinction and underlines a sense of excellence. The color on the tub's base is repeated on the top of the lid to complete the consistent and venerable presentation of the overall package.

FOO.GO PACKAGING

DESIGN
**THE FORMATION
CREATIVE CONSULTANTS**

CLIENT
GEORGE ROBINSON

052

SPECIFICATIONS
- ➔ Biodegradable paperboard
- ➔ Low-odor food-grade inks
- ➔ 36 μm PLA window

Packaging for fast food is frequently targeted by campaigners for being environmentally and socially detrimental, owing to its often relatively excessive use of resources and the way it regularly ends up as litter. Although packaging content and plenty of success has been gained in this area, recycling remains problematic for items that are consumed "on the go."

This renowned brand of convenience food has chosen to tackle the problem head-on by being the first to introduce an award-winning biodegradable food-grade packaging material that, in the right conditions, composts fully within 14 weeks. As a celebration of good honest food from locally sourced ingredients, this brand depends on ensuring that its environmental message touches every aspect of its business, including the packaging of its products. The biodegradable material provides a finish that is comparable to alternative, less environmentally sound, materials and can be printed using food-grade litho inks. The package is sealed using food-grade PVA adhesive and a combination of heat and pressure. The transparent window also boasts biodegradable qualities, and is made from 36 μm PLA.

The large window, which allows consumers to see the product within, is also manufactured from a fully biodegradable material, which is a recent innovation in the production of transparent plastics that at last gives designers an environmentally friendly alternative to using non-renewable and non-biodegradable alternatives.

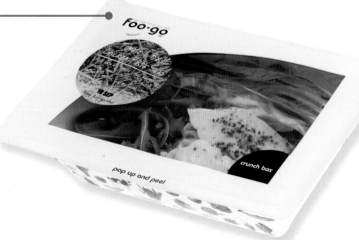

The wrap poses a particular problem for designers, owing to its shape, form, and the manner in which it is eaten. This popular food type therefore demands a bespoke design solution, which has been achieved successfully here with a compact, easily stackable, and, most importantly, biodegradable package.

MATTERIA CORPORATE IDENTITY AND BUSINESS CARDS

DESIGN	CLIENT
EMMI SALONEN	**MATTERIA**

SPECIFICATIONS
- ➔ Vegetable-based inks
- ➔ 100 percent recycled paper and cardboard, including 100 percent recycled Cairn Board

Designing the corporate identity for a shop specializing in ecological lifestyle products necessarily must respect, reflect, and live up to the environmental philosophy of that business. The graphic design for the brand was conceived to echo the cycles in nature, which appear as a series of circular devices, each divided into a varying number of segments by clean, crisp lines dissecting each circle. This theme not only bears an environmental message, but is also easily reproduced in any number of different forms and configurations across the company's printed material, such as stationery, marketing literature, and corporate packaging. These significantly different platforms provide a wide range of potential applications through which the brand can not only display this visual message, but also actively employ environmentally friendly materials and printing processes. This is true of all the company's printed material, which strives always to use recycled materials and non-synthetic inks.

GRID NOTEPADS

DESIGN
ASTRID STAVRO

CLIENT
**ROYAL COLLEGE OF ART,
MIQUELRIUS**

SPECIFICATIONS
➔ 100gsm Conqueror smooth ivory uncoated paper
➔ 3,000 micron gray cardboard

Astrid Stavro designed a series of seven different notepads that recreate grids that played a historic role in the development of design systems. These notepads cover a wide spectrum of classic and contemporary editorial design. Besides their role as historic "reminders" and homages, the notepads may be used for memo notes, doodling, shopping lists, writing letters, etc. Materials used include 100gsm Conqueror smooth ivory uncoated paper and 3,000 micron gray cardboard.

The series includes the following notepads/grids: Jan Tschichold, Le Corbusier, Willy Fleckhause, Josef Müller-Brockmann, Paul Rand, Johannes Gutenberg, and David Hillman.

055

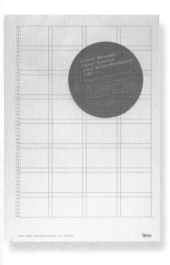

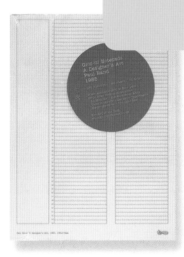

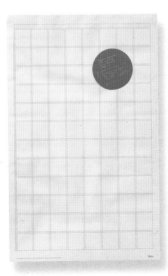

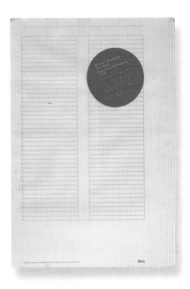

FLOCKS
PASSPORT

sheep collection fall/winter 2005

Uncoated stock has a rougher surface than coated stock. This quality allows it to absorb more ink, resulting in a duller, but pleasant look and feel. Uncoated paper is simply stock that has not been coated with china clay.

FLOCKS CORPORATE IDENTITY

DESIGN	CLIENT
JOLIAT	**FLOCKS**

SPECIFICATIONS
- 120gsm/200gsm Greentop crème
- White fabris
- Silver foil

Joliat created a corporate identity for the Swiss fashion brand FLOCKS. Each garment in the collection was produced from the wool of just one sheep, continuing until the wool was finished. A little passport of the sheep is attached to each jumper. Julia Joliat recalls, "Finding a flock of sheep wasn't as easy as it sounds; creating decent photography of sheep was even more difficult!" Materials used included 120gsm/200gsm Greentop creme and white fabris for the passport cover, which also used a silver foil for the title.

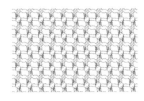

FLOCKS

Christian Meindertsma
Designer
Marconistraat 32
Haven 357
3029 AK Rotterdam
The Netherlands
+31 626 540 963
christian@theseflocks.com
www.theseflocks.com

LIBERTY INVITATION

DESIGN	CLIENT
MADETHOUGHT	**LIBERTY**

SPECIFICATIONS
- 16-panel folded sheet
- One-color printing
- Foil blocked

Produced as an invitation to celebrate a retail partnership with Liberty in London, this invite is formed from a single sheet of very thin bible paper folded down to a manageable format. The sheet is printed in black with a copper foil block used to highlight the event.

Also shown is an invitation for a UK launch during Design Week. This invite is a single sheet of grayboard, screen printed on both sides with white ink. Again, the company's logo is foil blocked in copper.

VITAM IMPENDERE VERO AND GRAJSKA ZAMETOVKA WINE LABELS

DESIGN
KROG, LJUBLJANA, SLOVENIA

SPECIFICATIONS
- Three-color lithography
- Foil blocking
- Laid paper

These two wine labels both use the same distinctive material and processes. The paper is a textured, laid stock, with an effect that was originally created by the wire marks that ran through the papermaker's mold. When the paper was allowed to dry, these were transferred in subtle "watermark" mode to the finished sheet. This material, combined with the use of gold foil blocking, is evocative of traditional high quality—a message that is conveyed by association to the wine contained in both bottles. These labels are both printed in three PANTONE colors using lithography, with tints used to expand the color range within the designs.

059

PASTICCINO DOLCE BOX AND TUBS

DESIGN
HELVETICA

CLIENT
HOTEL NIKKO TOKYO

SPECIFICATIONS
- ➔ Matte paper
- ➔ Matte varnish
- ➔ Gloss hot stamp

Designed for a renowned boutique hotel in Tokyo, this series of packages aims to evince the exclusive interior and luxurious atmosphere of the hotel. The product is comprised of four elements: the outer cartonboard container and three cylindrical drums that contain confectionary. Visual detailing has been kept to a minimum on the outer container, with only the product name and title appearing centrally among a series of vertical stripes of pale yellow and white. The finish is deliberately understated in order to allow the viewer to savor the more elaborately decorated packaging within. The three drums of confectionary sit side-by-side in the rectangular outer container. Duotone photographic imagery provides the predominant visual theme, setting the tone of the products and the sense of distinction of the establishment they represent. Each drum is made from dense fiberboard and contains a lid that can be removed by pulling on a fabric tag in the center of the top of the lid. The lids have been left white except for the printed text and logo, which duplicate the information on the front of the outer container.

A matte finish has been applied to the bases and lids of the cylindrical drums to convey a sense of simplicity and quality. In this case, the dense fiberboard, the quality of the photographic imagery, and the manner in which the lids smoothly slide from the bases of the cylinders suit a matte finish, so evoking a sense of quality and understated charm.

MATERIALS // GLOSS PAPER

HEFTI JEUNESSE CHOCOLATE BOX

DESIGN
HELVETICA

CLIENT
BÖÖGG JAPAN

SPECIFICATIONS
- Gloss paper
- Vacuum-formed plastic tray
- Transparent film

A combination of materials and finishes has been used to create an upscale appearance for a Swiss product aimed at a Japanese market. The two different sizes of package use the same design principle of a printed outer cartonboard container and an inner vacuum-molded plastic tray to securely house the products, which are kept fresh within a transparent, sealed plastic wrapping. A number of different production finishes are used in the three different materials that make up the package, but it is the printing finish that is primarily responsible for evoking the product's character and prominence. The range of sensuous brown tones in a striking pattern of different-sized crescents overlaid upon a base of deep chocolate-brown is highly suggestive of the product's alluring and appetizing characteristics. A large dark-brown circle with an inner circle of lighter brown provides a platform on which the product title and supplementary information can be displayed clearly but discreetly in white. A matte finish has been applied to the outer container to retain the textual quality of the cartonboard and to reflect the silky character of the product.

Plant this heart in your garden and wildflowers will blossom in memory of your loved one.

Plant this heart in your garden and wildflowers will blossom in memory of your loved one.

MATERIALS // COTTON PAPER

062

SEED PAPER

DESIGN AND CLIENT
NEW PALTZ GREENPARTY/MILSO INDUSTRIES

SPECIFICATIONS
● 100 percent cotton fiber embedded with wildflower seeds

Often the environmental credentials of a printed project are discernible only through small logos or taglines on the back of the product explaining how the printing technique or production process has helped to reduce the impact on the environment. Sometimes there is no evidence at all. This paper, however, goes to the other extreme and not only looks and feels environmentally sound because of its rough texture and speckled appearance, but actually germinates and flowers if planted somewhere that receives sunlight. The possibilities for this type of printing material are endless, but these two examples demonstrate two creative uses that exploit the obvious environmental message of this paper. One is a promotional postcard for an environmental party, while the other is a greetings card that encourages the user to plant the heart-shaped paper in memory of loved ones.

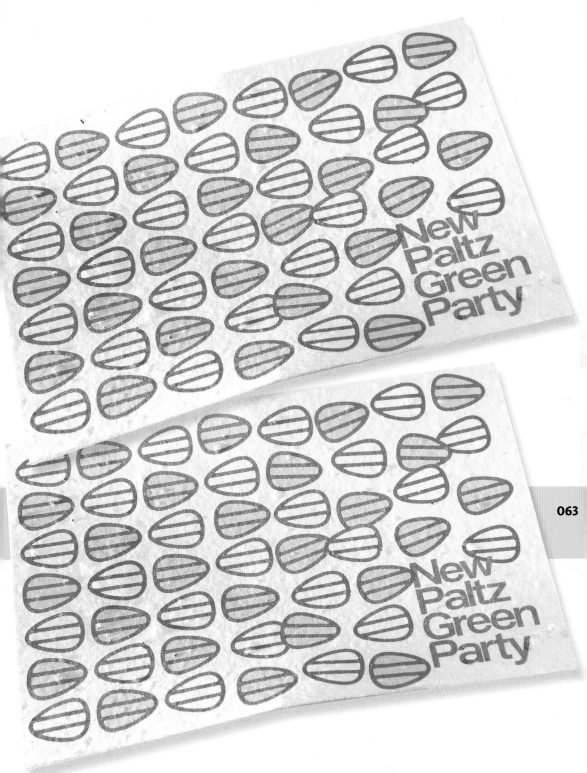

★ GREEN GOODS FOR MODERN DOGS ★

BUBBLE+SQUEAK

HERBAL DOG SHAMPOO

1   2   3

BASIC
FORMULA

WITH **ORGANIC PEPPERMINT,
LAVENDER, ROSEMARY
AND HEMP OIL**

A LITTLE GOES
A LONG WAY

GENTLE ON DOGS & THE EARTH

ECO-FRIENDLY   12 oz.   DETERGENT-FREE

Olive Heaven Scent

FUR
SPRITZER

Essential Oils of Lavender,
Lemon and Patchouli

4 fl. oz.

Elegant. Luxurious.
Tail-waggingly appealing.
When you don't have
time to go to the beauty
parlor, there's "Olive
Heaven Scent Fur Spritzer."
We blended natural,
essential oils of lavender,
lemon and patchouli to
create a distinctive, heaven-
ly scented spritzer that is
sure to delight the senses.
Your pooch will thank you.
Your pooch's friends will
thank you. And your couch
will thank you.

FOR MORE PRODUCTS TO LAVISH YOUR POOCH VISIT
OLIVEGREENDOG.COM

ECO- BRANDING AND PACKAGING

DESIGN
MODERN DOG

CLIENT
OLIVE, GREEN GOODS FOR MODERN DOGS

SPECIFICATIONS
- 100 percent PCW paper
- Soy-based inks
- Recyclable plastic

Designing a new identity for an environmentally dedicated online company that supplies the very best the internet has to offer in ecologically friendly, healthy, and groovy products for dogs is a rare and entertaining opportunity. The fun-loving and ecologically minded character of the business has been successfully encapsulated in the new identity and is reflected strongly through its online site. These own-brand products are designed specifically to reduce packaging content and all paper labeling is printed on 100 percent PCW paper using soy-based inks. For example, using bars of soap instead of plastic bottles keeps resources out of landfill or from even entering the recycling loop. Where plastic packaging has been used, it was chosen to be fully recyclable.

065

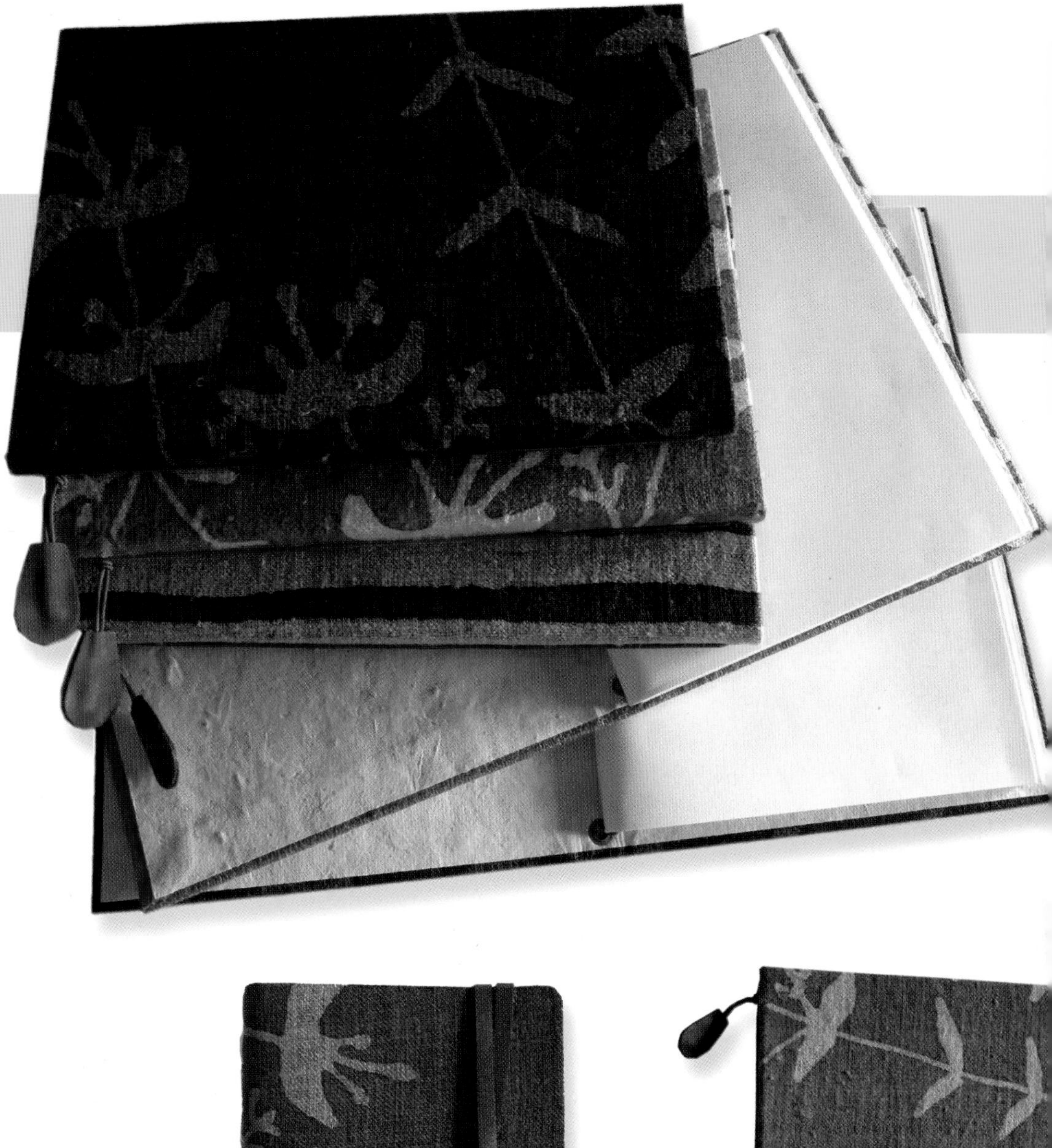

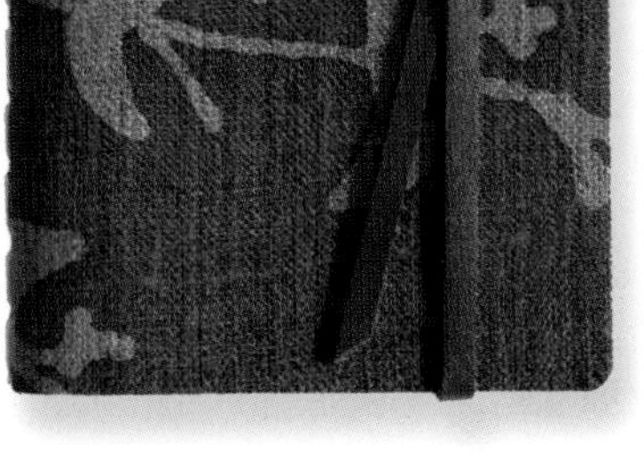

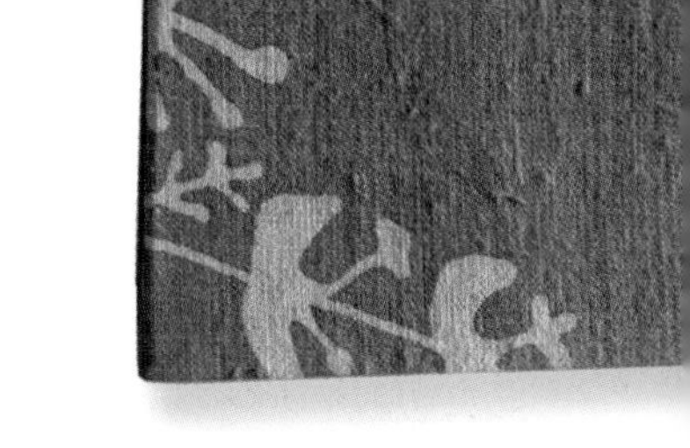

HEMP NOTEBOOKS

DESIGN	CLIENT
KATHY STEFANAC	**OIKO**

SPECIFICATIONS
➲ Hand-painted and hand-woven hemp covers
   with handmade paper leaves

Although notebooks are often small and seemingly inconsequential in terms of their environmental impact, they do represent an opportunity to be either an environmental burden or a potential boon. Collectively, if they use virgin paper and non-renewable resources in their printing or binding, they represent a significant drain on resources. However, their diminutive size also provides an opportunity to reuse waste material from other industries that might otherwise be disposed of. This series of notebooks is manufactured in South East Asia and is part of a brand founded on providing a useful and commercially viable channel for the skills and traditional practices of the Hmong ethnic group living in Laos and northern Vietnam. The covers are bound with off-cuts of hand-woven and hand-painted hemp manufactured for the production of larger products such as cushions, handbags, and other fashion accessories, giving the notebooks an exclusive and sensual finish. The leather tags and bookmarks are also byproducts of the production of handbags and wallets in this collection. Inside, the leaves are fabricated from traditionally handmade paper.

067

MINI MODERNS WALLPAPER RANGE

DESIGN
ABSOLUTE ZERO DEGREES

CLIENT
MINI MODERNS

SPECIFICATIONS
- Printed in the UK on FSC-certified paper
- Produced in Germany using water-based inks
  in one or two colors

When designing for the environment, half the battle is reducing obsolescence. So much of what we buy becomes redundant, outdated, or faulty long before the end of its useful life. If designers gave more attention to increasing the longevity of the products they create, then fewer resources would be used. In recent decades, designing for obsolescence seems to have become an unspoken, yet desirable objective by some desperate or irresponsible practitioners. However, if it's not the growing numbers of frustrated and dissatisfied consumers and clients that force a change to these unfortunate practices, it will be environmental necessity that imposes a change— we simply cannot go on producing mountains of waste to keep mediocre designers and manufacturers in business. Changing this mindset requires a greater appreciation for quality and a much better understanding of the true meaning of value.

The concept behind this range of wallpapers pays respect to these broader themes through a number of different designs for children that are deliberately fun, contemporary, and smart, yet mature and enduring. Each design is printed in one or two colors from a range including powder paint blue, smoothie pink, pear green, and milk chocolate, in various themes and motifs that are appropriate in the bedroom or playroom of a child of any age ("kids and kidults"!). The hugely popular designs are now sold around the world and have been shortlisted for interior design awards.

069

These wallpapers are produced by etching a roller in relief with a repeating pattern. The prints are designed to limit the amount of matching from seam to seam to make them easier to hang, so it might be the tip of anumeral, the wings of a bee, or the branch of a tree.

DVD REEL PACKAGING

DESIGN
PH.D

CLIENT
THE JONESES

SPECIFICATIONS
➲ Box with full wraparound wallpaper insert
➲ Adhesive label

Produced to promote commercial production company The Joneses, this DVD packaging reflects the individuality of the different directors, while sitting together as a set. Using cut-to-size retro wallpaper as a full wraparound insert, they instantly take us into the suburbs, and the world of "keeping up with the Joneses." With bold designs and colors, the kitsch wallpapers are visually striking, and the clear packs allow the different textures to show through.

While Ph.D initially thought that removing the need for print on the sleeve itself would reduce production costs, vintage wallpapers turned out to be "hellishly" expensive.

As a cost-effective way of naming the DVDs, Ph.D applied adhesive labels to the outside of the packaging. When lined up, the spines produce an appealing "library" effect.

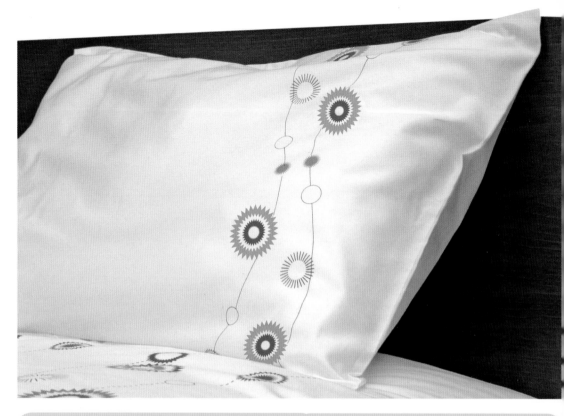

OLLI & LIME
INTERIORS RANGE

072

DESIGN/CLIENT
OLLI & LIME

SPECIFICATIONS
- ⊙ Wallpaper: two-color, flexoprint, top-coated
- ⊙ Fabrics: one-color screen print using 100 percent unbleached satin cotton

This range of products comprises a number of interior furnishings, including wallpaper, cushions, fabrics, and bedding, united by a series of distinctive designs that are both stylish and fun. Designed for a young market, these retro patterns are repeated across the soft furnishings range and embody the brand's philosophy, which strives to abandon the often patronizing approach to children's design, and instead aims to offer a series of alternatives that are clean, crisp, and can grow with the user. The stylish patterns, which appear in various natural tones of roasted brown, burnt orange, rich sage, and deep plum, are replicated throughout a choice of matching wallpaper in identical tones and playful motifs. Owing to this careful attention to detail, the life cycles of all the associated products are extended significantly, thereby preventing the unnecessary waste of precious resources.

All the fabrics in this range are screen printed using a one-color process and woven in a certified Fairtrade factory using 100 percent unbleached satin cotton.

The wallpaper is manufactured from wood sourced with the Finnish Forest Certification Scheme (FFCS), and printed in a two-color process using only one roller to reduce environmental impact. The factory pays additional charges to the local water board to ensure that the run-out from inks is cleaned thoroughly before returning to the water table.

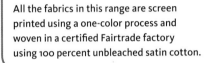

ROOT BEER BOTTLE

DESIGN/CLIENT
WHITE ROCK

SPECIFICATIONS
- Vitro cured ink
- Preprinted tray

A key benefit of glass packaging is that customized designs and branding can be applied to the surface of the bottle rather than being achieved through the design of the bottle itself. This significantly reduces costs while maintaining a high degree of design flexibility and quality. Many brands avoid the high setup costs of manufacturing bespoke molds and instead use standard molds, allowing them to invest in the design and application of labels and inks to the bottle's surface to deliver a strong visual message and reinforce brand imagery.

SENSPA BOTTLES

DESIGN
FLIPFLOP DESIGN

CLIENT
SENSPA

SPECIFICATIONS
➔ Silkscreen printing
➔ Spray painting

This range of products employs similar printing and production finishes across different packaging types to ensure a cohesive and coherent brand identity. The white floral pattern, subtly distinct for each product, appears in an analogous style and type of finish: silkscreen printed onto glass that has been tinted using an ink spray that gives the surface of the glass a textured matte finish. Screen printing directly onto glass eliminates the need for printed labels and, in this product range, enhances the overall appearance and perceived value of the packaging. The choice of plain white closures helps to maintain the purity and visual simplicity of each container.

075

The choice of rich earthy colors and the tactility produced by the matte finish are deliberate design choices made to reflect and maintain the brand's natural characteristics.

RHUBARB
SODA

DRY™

SODA: RHUBARB / 12 FL OZ (355 mL)
refreshingly tart and complex. all natural.

PRODUCED BY:

DRY SODA BOTTLES

DESIGN
TURNSTYLE

CLIENT
DRY SODA COMPANY

SPECIFICATIONS
- ➔ Screen printed label
- ➔ Cartonboard
- ➔ Offset lithography

The brand identity in this range of products has clearly translated across different materials and surfaces through the sympathetic use of separate printing techniques. The luscious hues that reflect the flavor and appearance of each product are offset against the liquid in the glass bottles. The screen printed labeling on the bottle has been kept to the minimum, maintaining the pure character of the product. This theme is continued to the bottle's carry case, where typography is applied sparsely and surfaces are bathed in the color that represents the product flavor.

The motif of bubbles, composed of five different-sized circles, is a clever and subtle unifying detail repeated across three material finishes: the cartonboard carry case, the glass bottle, and the metal crown cap.

LAVENDER
SODA

KUMQUAT
SODA

MACALLAN WHISKY BOTTLE

DESIGN
DESIGN BRIDGE

CLIENT
MACALLAN WHISKY

078

SPECIFICATIONS
➔ Molded glass
➔ Woodturning

The purity and preeminence of the product is lovingly revered in this design, which uses a number of distinguished finishes to set it apart from potential competitors. This has been achieved through a combination of the physical design, choice of materials and printing finishes. The physical character of the glass bottle is most distinctive, its bulbous, organic form so markedly different from the often formal range of geometric shapes used by similar products in the market. Crowning this curvaceous body is the equally eye-catching feature of the wooden screwcap that has been turned to have a slight swelling and rounded top that matches the shapely nature of the glass bottle beneath. The printed graphics provide the exceptional finishing touches. The textural quality of the leaves' skeletal structure is created by the white print contrasting with the rich tones of the whisky. Furthermore, this design is continued on the back of the bottle, so that from any angle the shadowy motif can be seen through the liquid, giving the whole package a sense of depth and reinforcing the brand's eminent identity.

MINIATURE LIQUOR BOTTLES

DESIGN
RICE DESIGN

CLIENT
SUNTORY CO. LTD.

SPECIFICATIONS
➤ Metallic adhesive paper label
➤ Etched glass
➤ ROPP screw caps

Distinctive printing finishes have been applied to both the labels and the caps of this range of miniature bottles to create a strong brand image as well as a bold individual appearance in each design. The vivid hues of the central portion of the label, repeated in the text as well as in a metallic finish on the cap, display a bright and refreshing message that is augmented by the icy freshness of the silver printing behind and the frosted glass of the bottle. The names of each product appear in a large typeface printed in white and inlaid in the silver background. The frosted glass is created during the manufacturing process to create a textured finish that is both physically intriguing and visually appealing.

079

LAKRITSI TIN

DESIGN
GLUD & MARSTRAND

CLIENT
OY HALVA AB

SPECIFICATIONS
➔ Black ink veneer
➔ Stamping

080

On this package, a veneer of soft black ink on metal provides the foundation for a lucid appearance that boasts exceptional clarity of printed graphics. The choice of printing finish and the shape of the container have been chosen to intimate the product contained within, and, in so doing, produce a tactile effect and an almost edible evocation of the silky surface finish of licorice. With such a bold black background there is no need for subtle hints and gradients in the printing, which would only detract from the eminent simplicity of the overall concept. Instead, all fonts and graphics are boldly stamped onto the surface in just two colors plus white to create a dramatic illustration that upholds the exclusiveness of a product targeted at the discerning customer. The material and its untainted surface texture are essential to the success of the whole composition, visually and tactilely, as well as to the phenomenal success in the marketplace in which it experienced a threefold increase in sales since the redesign.

The decision to replace previous foil-bag packaging with a metal tin was one not only aimed at making a statement about exclusivity in a highly competitive market, but was also a marketing decision that acknowledged the fact that users would keep the package and that its reuse would serve as a marketing device long after its contents had been consumed.

The characteristics of the material have been used to create the opening device for the package, which requires the application of pressure to lever the lid from the base. The functional role of this device has been visually marked in the physical form of the package, with the simple instruction "Press" embossed into the surface of the lid.

MATERIALS // METAL

ALTOIDS TIN

DESIGN
CROWN HOLDINGS, INC.

CLIENT
CALLARD & BOWSER

SPECIFICATIONS
➔ Embossing

Metal packaging possesses a quality that can be hard to match using other packaging materials. Not only can it be forged during the production process to create all manner of appealing shapes, but the quality of its surface makes it an exceptional platform on which to display product information attractively. This world-famous brand uses the material properties of metal to create a physically and visually striking container. The two-part container is largely unadorned on the base, but the lid has been shaped to present a surface on which the product title and brand information is charmingly presented through a combination of production and printing finishes. Embossing has been used to help the brand name stand out from the surface of the container both figuratively and actually, augmented by the choice of printing that appears in a circle on the surface of the lid. It has been left bare over the embossing so that the sheen of the metal surface is used to highlight this particular facet of the package.

HOLISTIC BEAU-TEA SACHET

082

DESIGN
HELVETICA

CLIENT
NATURAL HOUSE

SPECIFICATIONS
- ➔ Matte paper
- ➔ Matte seal
- ➔ Metal foil
- ➔ Adhesive label

Minimalism and freshness are the cornerstones of this packaging for a tea aimed at the natural-food market. The packaging finishes aim to reflect the distinctive characteristics of Japanese culture, both in their appearance and in their physical qualities. The thick foil bag presents a distinctive and eye-catching appearance while also evoking a sense of hygiene and product freshness. Product information and branding are displayed on a simple adhesive label printed in organic tones that depicts the natural qualities of the product. Innovations in production techniques have allowed the bag to be resealable using a zipper along the length of the top, which helps keep the product fresh.

The unadorned and silky texture of the foil bag uses the unique characteristics of metal to provide a tactile finish suggestive of hygiene and quality.

TAB

タブを手前におこし、右に引っぱって下さい。

ZIPPER

HOLISTIC BEAU-TEA　　Oregon Tilth 認証ハーブ100％使用

Natural House

ハーバリストが厳選した7種のハーブのブレンドティ

Reset Blend
リセットブレンド

7包入

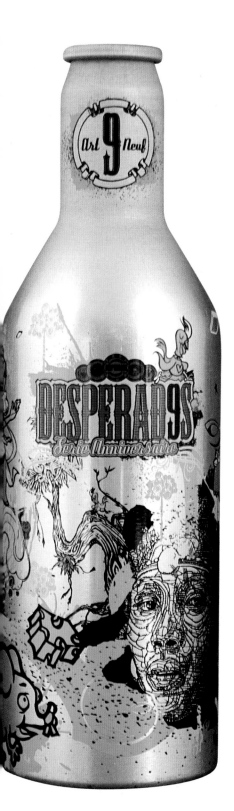

DESPERADOS BOTTLES

DESIGN	CLIENT
BOXAL	**BRASSERIE FISCHER**

SPECIFICATIONS
- Six-color dry offset
- Brushed aluminum substrate
- Gloss varnish

Only a few years ago, bottles used for the commercial packaging of liquids were almost always made from glass or, occasionally, ceramics. This established status quo has been radically shaken since the advent of the metal bottle. Elaborately shaped aluminum bottles were previously unthinkable, but with advances in manufacturing technologies it is not only possible to manufacture bottles from a single piece, it is also cheap. This atypical packaging medium—so easily distinguishable from its main competitor, glass—offers customers a unique experience through the material's characteristic qualities, which, in turn, helps to boost brand recognition. Metal packaging is also a versatile medium on which to apply printed graphics, thereby further enhancing the package's already excellent characteristics. Here, three different designs for a range of drinks demonstrate the extremely high-definition print finish, using a six-color process, that can be applied to the surface of metal bottles. The same level of detail is not possible on the surface of glass, other than by using shrink sleeves or labels.

083

GIORGIO DAVANZO CARDS

084

DESIGN/CLIENT
GIORGIO DAVANZO

SPECIFICATIONS
❯ Photo-etching on aluminum

Giorgio Davanzo Design's self-promotional hangtag makes very unusual use of materials and processes: it is produced from a fine sheet of polished aluminum, with the design and information photo-etched into the surface. Lucky recipients are bound to be impressed by this highly crafted and precise keepsake, made from a different and unexpected material. Consequently, they are likely to attribute the quality of precise craftsmanship to its creators.

The combination of material and processes gives the impression of a beautifully produced decorative piece, as the photo-etching has not only cut finely crafted, closely spaced small holes, but also engraved the details of a complex weather map into the satin-smooth surface of the tag.

PABHAUS BRANDING

DESIGN
INKSURGE

CLIENT
PABLO GALLERY

SPECIFICATIONS
- Ceramic tiles
- Narra wood
- Canvas with digital printing and laser etching

Inksurge is a collective design studio (based in Manila, Philippines) that enjoys working on any form of experimental design. It was therefore a perfect brief for Inksurge when it was asked to brand and create work for Pabhaus, a graphic design/furniture show featuring Manila's graphic design talents. The materials used to make up the branding included ceramic tiles, Narra wood, and canvas with digital printing and laser etching.

To create these intricate patterns out of solid wood, hand carving simply would not be cost-effective. Laser etching is a very precise method of creating highly intricate shapes and still retaining a hand-carved look.

These cards combine richly colored Italian paper, little discs of sustainably harvested wood, as well as offcuts and misprints from the company's own lines of letterpress and wooden cards, making each card truly unique and providing an excellent way to reuse materials.

NIGHT OWL PAPER GOODS STATIONERY

DESIGN	CLIENT
ALAN HENDERSON AND JENNIFER TATHAM	**NIGHT OWL PAPER GOODS**

SPECIFICATIONS
- ➔ FSC-certified 100 percent post-consumer recycled paper, processed chlorine-free
- ➔ Sustainably harvested birch
- ➔ Douglas fir
- ➔ Walnut

This range of stationery incorporates very thinly cut wood for the covers and the base boards of some of its products, including journals, notebooks, greetings cards, and calendars. Inspired by all things produced by nature, the designers of this stationery range have combined natural materials with elegant designs based on environmental themes, including the company logo of two owls on the limb of a branch. Reflecting the company's passion for craftsmanship and detail, the evolved style of these designs, employing a delicate use of color, texture, and pattern to create bespoke products, is referred to as "modern, yet folksy."

Different types of wood, including sustainably harvested birch, walnut, and Douglas fir, provide the raw materials for the covers, while paper manufactured from 100 percent post-consumer waste is used for the pages and the paper leaves of the notepads. Unlike recycled or virgin paper, finely sliced wood uses no water in its production and requires much less energy. The result is a distinctive product with a unique grain and texture that cannot fail to catch the eye—each one an inimitable piece of art.

The pages are manufactured from 100 percent post-consumer recycled paper and spiral-bound with the cover, which is produced from eco-friendly sustainably harvested birch. For every tree felled, another is replanted. The floral design is applied to the cover using standard inks, which have been chosen for their durability.

This calendar is manufactured entirely from three different types of sustainably harvested wood. With one month printed on each face, the calendar comprises six pages printed on the front and rear and spiral bound along the top edge. Encasing the six pages is a slightly larger cover, also produced in wood, that also serves as a stand.

BIRTHDAY INVITATIONS

DESIGN
THE MILITARY

CLIENT
REBECCA FLOUNDERS

SPECIFICATIONS
- ➔ Plasterboard
- ➔ Stamping
- ➔ Rubber die

With a production run of just 90, these hand-finished invitations consisted of cut plasterboard sections with stamped artwork. They were created using 9mm (c. ⅜in) British Gypsum Handi-board and a simple rubber die and pad.

Once The Military had decided on the plasterboard format, it wanted to emulate precisely the dot matrix copy on the back of the gypsum sheets for the information on the front. The copy looked as though it had been applied to the sheets in a very quick motion in the factory and had a slight lean to it.

For small print runs, a rubber die is a reasonably cheap, effective, and fun way of printing onto awkward or unusual materials. A rubber die with the text cast onto its surface is inked up and stamped onto the material to create handpressed printing.

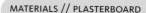

MATERIALS // RUBBER

MTV MEDIA SALES PRESENTATION PACKAGING

DESIGN	CLIENT
BLAST	**MTV GLOBAL**

SPECIFICATIONS
➔ Screen printed heat-sealed embossed rubber

Blast wanted to reflect the modernity of MTV in this project and inspiration came in the form of plastics samples received prior to being commissioned. The agency felt that the rubber echoed this modernity, and the use of different colored materials also suggested diversity. The main constraint on the project was that the packaging had to be fairly generic as each case would house a bespoke presentation. So Blast chose to use a global atlas graphic, but styled in an unusual and modern way, and embossed for a little more subtlety.

This packaging makes interesting use of a material not widely used in CD packaging—rubber. The embossing is clean and simple and, as the agency says, makes the whole piece rather tactile or "touchy feely."

TONY WILLIAMS LIFETIME CD SET

090

DESIGN	CLIENT
GIULIO TURTURRO	**VERVE RECORDS**

SPECIFICATIONS
- Two-CD jewel case
- Clear vinyl slipcase printed in two colors
- 16-page saddle-stitched booklet on uncoated stock

Inspired by the music of Tony Williams, who drummed for the likes of Miles Davis, Giulio Turtorro's primary aim was to produce a slipcase that simulated the skin of a drum. The budget was slightly above average, but Giulio chose to hold back on color in the booklet so that he could splurge on the slipcase. In addition, having the insert in black-and-white meant it didn't detract from the slipcase, the main focal point of the packaging. The only color is on the inner tray at the back, which you glimpse through the transparent areas of the slipcase print. The drumming theme is echoed in the back cover and inner tray, with overlaid circles representing the floor plan of a drum kit. Retro touches such as the graphics, fonts, and the concentric circles on the CD—resembling old-fashioned vinyl—allude to the artist's 1970s music.

The two-color print and transparent areas of this slipcase create an interesting effect. It's particularly unusual for a design to obscure both the face of the artist and the album's track listing, but it adds an element of intrigue.

DJ SPINNA CD PACKAGING

DESIGN
CRUSH DESIGN

CLIENT
URBAN THEORY

SPECIFICATIONS
- CD gatefold
- Triple vinyl box

Taking a fresh approach to graffiti graphics, Crush's design for DJ Spinna's album features a 1950s-style illustration of two women in the "control room"—the designer's interpretation of the album's title The Beat Suite. Printed in a vibrant red, the T-shape gatefold packaging has simple die-cut slots to hold the CDs, and sits inside the outer slipcase.

The gatefold CD holder uses a T-shaped format to allow extra space for the graphics. The quarters, in which the CDs sit within the die-cuts are left unusually blank, thus not distracting from the bold, black-and-gold CD designs.

REUSED ENVELOPE TAPE

DESIGN/CLIENT
EMMI SALONEN

SPECIFICATIONS
➔ Adhesive tape

Reducing the environmental impact of products or packaging through the innovative use and application of certain finishes can often demand inventive or even quirky decision-making. This example, though not boasting rigorous environmental credentials itself, has been devised to improve the environmental credentials of other products and packaging. All businesses get inundated with envelopes and other types of secondary packaging and much of this gets thrown away or, if the business is environmentally concerned enough, recycled. However, an improvement on recycling is for this secondary packaging to be reused. This can often be a time-consuming process concluding with an unattractive result whose patchwork character is likely to shame the sender, regardless of their good environmental intentions. This roll of adhesive tape has been designed to overcome this common problem and provide an attractive method of reusing old envelopes with a finish that is smart, clean, and tasteful. Despite extensive efforts, no printer could be found that could print vegetable-based inks on the plastic surface of the adhesive tape, but it is hoped that such a technique will be developed in the future.

Subtle graphic imagery and text not only makes the recipient aware that the packaging has been reused, but also serves as an ideal platform for corporate promotion and advertising.

STANDARD
PRINTING

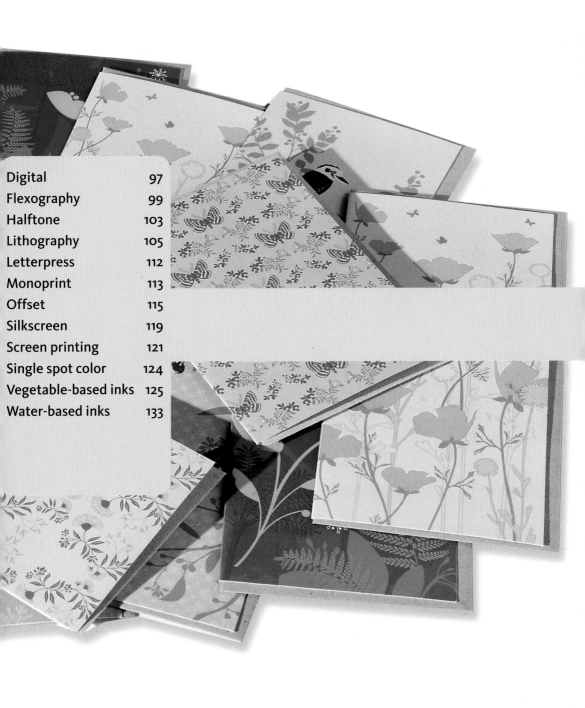

SELF-PROMOTIONAL MAILER

DESIGN/CLIENT
EMMI

SPECIFICATIONS
- 100 percent recycled Colorset Ash
- Sappi Heritage recycled stock
- Neptune Unique paper
- Rubber band

This mailer self-promoting the work of London designer Emmi Salonen can be tailored for specific prospective clients. The mailer consisted of two sections (yellow and white), each of which was bound within a "shell" of 100 percent recycled Colorset Ash using a rubber band.

The yellow section, which was on a Sappi Heritage recycled stock, can be updated by laser printing in a single black. The other full-color section printed on Neptune Unique paper can be reordered depending on the recipient (book for publishers, CD for record companies, etc.).

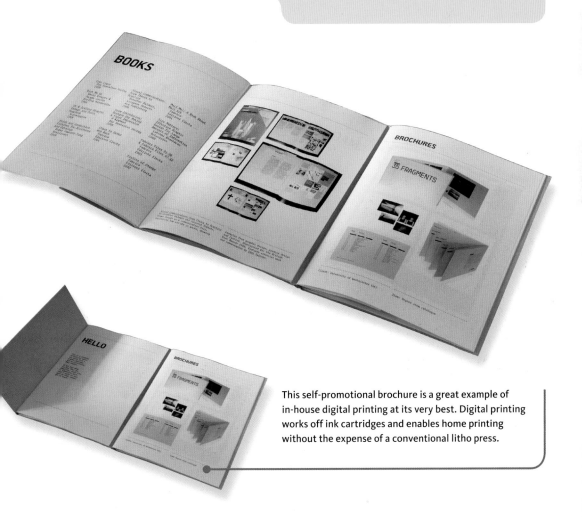

This self-promotional brochure is a great example of in-house digital printing at its very best. Digital printing works off ink cartridges and enables home printing without the expense of a conventional litho press.

CONCRETE HERMIT CATALOG

DESIGN
EMMI SALONEN

CLIENT
CONCRETE HERMIT

SPECIFICATIONS
➔ Digital printing

Obsolescence is one of those unavoidable attributes of design that is seldom highlighted when seeking environmental improvements. While printing and production processes are vital factors in reducing the environmental impact of design, increasing the life cycle of a product is arguably more beneficial.

This has been carefully considered in the case of this catalog for a London-based shop and gallery, the products of which inevitably have a high turnover. The decision to design a refillable format was both economic and environmental. The A5-sized (148 × 210mm/5¾ × 8¼in) catalog is also designed to be printed digitally, therefore eliminating the need for litho printing plates. Individual pages can be reprinted and replaced without having to reprint the entire document from scratch, which would be the case if it were bound using a permanent binding, thereby eliminating considerably potential waste. A durable cover manufactured from thick card encases the paper pages; its dark tone helps to conceal potential blemishes that might occur over the extended lifetime of the catalog.

LEMON JELLY BAGS

DESIGN
AIRSIDE

CLIENT
LEMON JELLY

SPECIFICATIONS
➔ Single-color flexography

Airside used a standard method of printing, flexography, to customize this small, bright yellow bag for the band Lemon Jelly. The piece was printed in single-color black, and the designers went out of their way to create an item that was "directly reminiscent of slightly 'tacky' children's party bags," explains Airside's Anne Brassier. The color of the bag was also carefully selected, reinforcing this concept and reassuring the recipient that they are bound to have a great time at a Lemon Jelly gig.

100

CALISTOGA BAKERY CAFE BAGS AND LABELS

DESIGN
VRONTIKIS DESIGN OFFICE

CLIENT
CALISTOGA BAKERY CAFE

SPECIFICATIONS
- Labels: three-color lithography
- Bags: four-color flexography, lamination

The distinctive, rich, earthy color palette remains consistent throughout every separate element that makes up Vrontikis Design Office's work for the Calistoga Bakery Cafe, yet each standalone item features well-considered and varied use of shifting color priority. Bags and labels are printed using two standard methods, depending upon which material is to be printed: paper-based products have been created using lithography, whereas silky-smooth, laminated foil coffee bags are produced using the most suitable process for their surface—flexography. These bags are first printed in white to provide a base that will enhance the quality of the remaining colors.

The selection of three PANTONE colors has provided the Calistoga Bakery Cafe with considerable design scope with which to differentiate their products. Each color has sufficient depth and density to hold even small serif typography without compromising legibility. The basic palette of red, yellow, and brown is occasionally supplemented with deep blue, but the design still remains true to the economy and visual character created by the three-color print palette.

The complementary combination of earthy shades, simply yet beautifully printed in litho and flexography, blends fluidly with the varied color priority. This not only helps add significant value to Calistoga Bakery Cafe products, but also helps to reinforce the impression that product and service possess the same degree of quality, consideration, care, and attention to detail that is present within the design.

BALLANTINE'S BOTTLE AND CARTON

DESIGN
DRAGON

CLIENT
PERNOD RICARD

SPECIFICATIONS
- Cartonboard
- Pressure-sensitive label
- Foil blocking
- Satin silver ink
- Halftone overprinting
- Embossing
- Offset lithography
- Lacquer varnish

Maintaining the strong brand presence of a distinguished product in a global marketplace is a major challenge for structural and graphic designers. The subtle redesign of this glass bottle and labeling used a range of finishes to successfully develop the brand's customer appeal and premium values in an international context. The glass bottle, with its broad facade, wide shoulders, and pronounced neck, projects a confident and sincere appearance that is augmented by the linear arrangement of printed labels and the distinctive pewter coin. The labels display the product logo and title clearly, using foil and satin silver printing to lift certain details from the various motifs, such as the elaborate crest and the labels' edging. Consideration for a broad range of different user environments has resulted in careful attention to detail in the labels' overall finish: a lacquer coating applied to the label not only enhances its appearance, but also makes it particularly conspicuous when lit with ultraviolet light such as that frequently used in bars or nightclubs. Printing finishes are vital in providing a premium feel to the secondary packaging, which comprises a litho-printed carton-board container. The product logo has been blind embossed on the side of the carton, while satin silver inks and halftone overprinting significantly improve the appearance of subtle elements such as the embossed coin.

The overall distinction of both the bottle and the carton is amplified by the coin device, which was achieved comparatively simply on the carton through printing and embossing, but which required rigorous testing before a suitable design solution for the bottle was found. The resulting pressure-sensitive label has been printed with subtle halftones to give the coin its graphic detailing, while a tactile varnish provides a subtly embossed feel to match the physical and visual elegance of the corresponding device on the carton.

The glossy surface of the carrier bag heightens the impact of the linear color against black, and adds the interplay of reflections to the distinct visual character of this Neiman Marcus promotion.

NEIMAN MARCUS BAGS

DESIGN
STEVEN WILSON

CLIENT
NEIMAN MARCUS

SPECIFICATIONS
➔ Four-color lithography

Brightly colored line drawings set against a dramatic, contrasting black background create very exciting and stylish promotional bags, postcards, and gift cards in this in-store promotion for Neiman Marcus.

Full color has been exploited to best effect with each hue being formed from only two colors from the CMYK process. This gives the printing a purity and clarity, enabling a special vibrancy to be achieved; more colors are inclined to "muddy" the colorful effect.

The sophisticated design and print interpretation produces a vivacious style while maintaining high-end market appeal. The linear illustrations create a sensitively balanced proportional relationship between image and background, and this allows an effective combination of vitality and finesse.

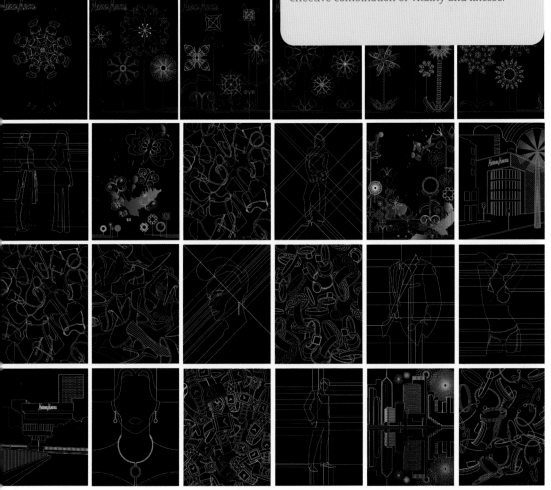

106

GALERIE AU CHOCOLAT LABELS

DESIGN
PAPRIKA

CLIENT
GALLERIE AU CHOCOLAT

SPECIFICATIONS
➔ Four-color lithography

Paprika's labels for Galerie au Chocolat indicate the product details cleanly and have great visual impact on the shelf. Designs were printed in four-color litho and make full use of the potential of this process. This includes the creation of specific full-color mixes to capture individual shades; the accurate reproduction of photographic imagery; and the printing of subtle, tinted background shades. With this printing method, all this can happen at the same time, using only four passes on press.

VINTAGE PEANUTS HANGTAGS

DESIGN
MSLK

SPECIFICATIONS
➔ Four-color lithography

The spirit of this clothing line seeks to capture the essence of the Peanuts brand from 1962–1968. Emotionally, the graphics are intended to make the viewer feel as if they are wearing a well-loved sweatshirt or a pair of jeans that are slightly worn around the edges. Although the hangtag is printed in regular four-color offset litho to create a believable vintage feel, MSLK produced printouts of label designs, then crumpled and physically distressed them before scanning the resulting weathered and "aged" effect for the artwork. The four-color process, printed on an absorbent, uncoated stock, has successfully captured the subtleties of the color scheme and textures of vintage labeling.

The designers at MSLK used Photoshop to create the slightly misregistered feel of the Snoopy and Woodstock illustrations, with background color and texture being enhanced by including a larger than normal dot-screen pattern. Using litho printing on absorbent, uncoated stock, these print effects cleverly conjure the less refined printing of Peanuts cartoons back in the 1960s.

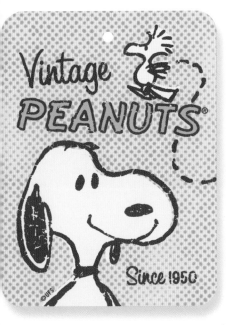

PEOPLE ARE PEOPLE BAGS

DESIGN
INKSURGE

CLIENT
PEOPLE ARE PEOPLE

SPECIFICATIONS
→ Four-color offset lithography
→ Coated stock
→ Gloss varnish

108

Inksurge printed distinctive illustrations on carrier bags for fashion store People are People. Gloss varnish was applied overall to give each bag a high-shine surface. By using the four-color process, all bags could be printed on the same print run and still have a distinctly focused color theme and a clear individuality.

Careful blending of combinations of cyan, magenta, yellow, and black has produced vivid shades of blue-green, pink, and yellow.

RED CAR WINE COMPANY LABELS

DESIGN
VRONTIKIS DESIGN OFFICE

CLIENT
RED CAR WINE COMPANY

SPECIFICATIONS
- ➔ Four-color lithography
- ➔ Uncoated stock

Excellent-quality four-color litho captures the subtleties of the illustrations that theme the Red Car Wine Company labels. The distinctive label for each vintage is used to perpetuate a long-running story that is portrayed using a specialist style of illustration. Within the featured label for The Table, scanning and print have captured the subtleties of changes in depth created by the original collaged illustration. This conjures a tactile quality that suggests to potential purchasers that the wine is not only handmade, but also hand-labeled, especially for their individual enjoyment.

Letterpress is a very traditional practice of printing from an inked, raised surface. In this case, using wooden blocks with an aged, damaged surface gives the range of stationery a fantastic and imperfect look and feel.

TOTAL CONTENT STATIONERY

DESIGN	CLIENT
NB: STUDIO	**TOTAL CONTENT**

SPECIFICATIONS
- GF Smith 150gsm and 350gsm Colorplan Pristine White stock
- Letterpress printing in double-hit PANTONE 805U 2X

Copywriters Total Content needed a set of new stationery. NB:Studio's design took its cue from the company name and features the total contents of a copywriter's most basic everyday tool, the alphabet. Character and punctuation symbols were placed in a variety of different fonts to reflect the different personalities and styles of Total Content's writing. All stationery items were letterpress printed to give a crafted look and feel and make each item individual. Fluro Orange was used to reflect the company's Dutch heritage.

Materials included GF Smith's 150gsm and 350gsm Colorplan Pristine White. Printing was by letterpress printing both sides in double-hit PANTONE 805U 2X.

Monoprinting is a classic example of excellent design using the cheapest possible methods of reproduction (photocopying) to achieve outstanding results.

ONE CLUB POSTER

DESIGN	CLIENT
IAMALWAYSHUNGRY	**ONE CLUB**

SPECIFICATIONS
➔ Photocopying on thick and thin stock

The One Club of New York approached Iamalwayshungry to create a poster for their show titled "Peace," and let the designers decide the poster's theme as well as its size and overall format. With the sheer amount of material President Bush has created, they chose to make him the voice of the piece, using a whole side for quotes primarily attributed to him.

Iamalwayshungry printed a limited run on a thick stock and actually decided to print the remainder on a cheaper thinner stock found at the local copy/mail center.

113

The Annual Weekly Planner has been designed so that the user can compile a series of planners into an annual volume, rather than purchasing an entire planner at the beginning of the year and not filling it, resulting in a considerable waste of resources.

LONG-LIFE PLANNERS

DESIGN
**LART COGNAC BERLINER;
SARAH LANNAN; MARTINE
WORKMAN; JEREMY CROWN;
YVONNE CHEN**

CLIENT
LITTLE OTSU

SPECIFICATIONS
- Four-color lithography
- Offset printing with soy-based inks
- 100 percent post-consumer recycled paper
- Chipboard back cover
- Spiral bound

Small details in design can often make a big difference to the environmental impact of a product. This pair of attractive and distinctive weekly planners have a number of well-considered details that affect the product's finish and help to reduce its environmental footprint. While planners, diaries, and journals are usually printed with set dates, which render them obsolete before the end of their useful life, these planners have deliberately omitted any fixed dates, leaving the user to insert their own dates and thereby helping to extend the life of the product indefinitely. The use of one-color process on the internal pages reduces the quantity of inks needed for the job, while maintaining the quality of the illustrations, which are rendered in pencil. Conversely, the pencil renderings on the cover have been printed using a four-color process to maintain a colorful and striking appearance.

All inks are soy-based and applied using an offset process, printed on 100 percent recycled paper manufactured from post-consumer waste. An uncoated recyclable matte metal spiral bind has been chosen for the binding so that the journals can be laid flat on a surface, allowing the whole week to appear horizontally across the double-page spread.

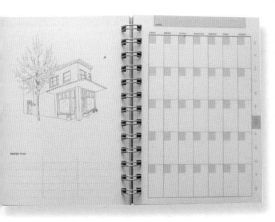

little otsu presents

the tour diary

by allison cole

a travel Companion

To keep costs down and reduce the quantity of ink used, the cover has been printed using a four-color process, while the internal pages are all printed in a single color.

TOUR DIARY

DESIGN
ALLISON COLE; JEREMY CROWN; YVONNE CHEN

CLIENT
LITTLE OTSU

SPECIFICATIONS
- Offset printing
- Soy-based inks
- 100 percent post-consumer recycled paper
- Bound using animal-free adhesives

Increasingly, the impact that travel has on the environment is causing people to become more aware about how, when, where, and for what reason they travel. This attractive travel diary is designed for the fun-seeking traveler who likes to consider every detail of their itinerary so that their environmental impact is as modest as possible—right down to the diary in the pocket. Printed using soy inks on uncoated 100 percent recycled post-consumer waste paper, the diary uses a delightful graphic design style printed in four colors to generate a bright and playful appearance. The diary's tall and lightweight format and perfect binding (which uses animal-free adhesives) ensures that it is easy to carry and store.

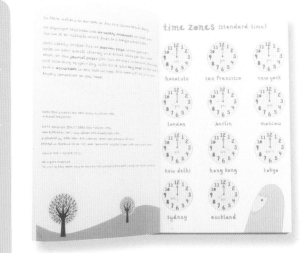

The paper for the cover and the internal pages has been deliberately left uncoated so as to improve the journal's recyclability and biodegradability. This also augments the design on the cover, which retains the sensual texture of the recycled material, and in turn echoes the rough plywood surface that has been reproduced with great accuracy.

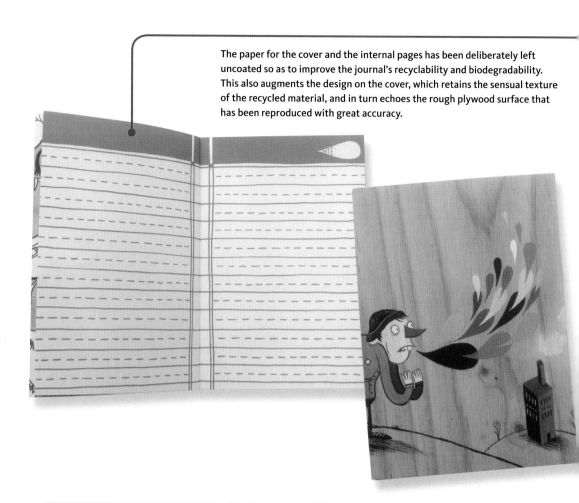

STANDARD PRINTING // OFFSET

ARTISTIC JOURNAL

DESIGN	CLIENT
JEREMY TINDER; JEREMY CROWN; YVONNE CHEN	**LITTLE OTSU**

SPECIFICATIONS
- Offset printing with soy-based inks
- 100 percent post-consumer recycled paper
- Bound with animal-free adhesives

Rather than manufacturing a journal solely for the purpose of note-taking, this design concept adopts a magnanimous approach, taking a piece of artwork from a reputable artist and reproducing it on the cover, thereby making the art affordable and easily available to a wide audience. This helps to ensure that when the journal reaches the end of its useful life, the cover at least lives on as a valued product in its own right. So as not to undermine the benevolent approach with poor environmental credentials, this journal has also been printed on paper manufactured from 100 percent post-consumer waste, uses only soy-based inks, and is bound using animal-free adhesives.

INTERNATIONAL WOMEN'S DAY MARKETING

DESIGN
SUPERBACANA DESIGN

CLIENT
ALMAP BBDO

SPECIFICATIONS
- ➜ Paper box
- ➜ Pure silk pouches, silkscreened
- ➜ 250gsm Duo Design paper
- ➜ 200gsm Translucents Orange
- ➜ Four-color offset

The advertising agency Almap BBDO commissioned Superbacana Design to make its relationship marketing item for International Women's Day. The gift consists of a small paper box with four small pure silk pouches with silkscreen print, suitable for organizing loose objects. Materials used included 250gsm Duo Design paper and 200gsm Translucents Orange with printing in four-color offset.

119

Silkscreen printing is a traditional form of printing by which ink is forced through a stencil glued to a taut screen. This is a particularly good method for printing onto fabrics, boards, or anything that is not able to be fed through a conventional printing press.

SENOK TEA LABELING AND POINT OF PURCHASE

DESIGN
GIORGIO DAVANZO DESIGN

CLIENT
SENOK TEA

SPECIFICATIONS
- Single-color screen printing
- Aluminum sheet
- Clear satin finish

Three-dimensional point-of-purchase design can be crafted using many different materials; this display is fabricated out of 16-gauge aluminum, and is coated with a layer of clear anodized satin finish. The display was screen printed in single color with brand information.

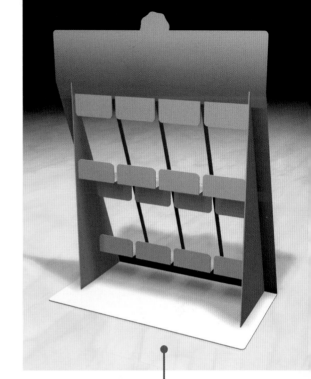

This image shows the structure of the design, highlighting cuts and folds that create precisely sized and located positioning for the products. The use of this durable metallic material tells potential buyers that Senok produces a high-quality, fresh, contemporary, stylish drink.

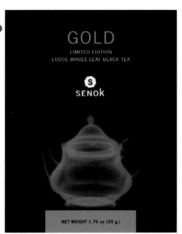

Senok's Gold and Silver tea labels are used to customize tea tins, and are each produced using two-color litho print on high-gloss crack-back label material. Each variety is printed in black, plus one PANTONE metallic color. This combination achieves a metallic quality not unlike that already seen on Senok's point of sale.

**3 kunstenaars actief
in Kunsthuis 7X11**

Bert van Ommen's Kunstuitleen
Collages van Ypenburgse architectuur
Expositie: laatste weekend van januari
en eerste weekend van februari 2005

Suze May Sho
'Cross-overs' van ontwerpers met
kunstwerken in een diashow
Expositie: laatste twee weekenden
van februari en de eerste twee van
maart 2005

PJ Roggeband
Langs de rand van Ypenburg
Expositie: april 2005

7X11 wordt wisselend bewoond door
kunstenaars die diverse projecten
realiseren voor en met bewoners
van Ypenburg. Deze kunstenaars
maken hun gedachtegoed en ideeën
zichtbaar in acties, confrontaties,
voorstellingen, publicaties en lezingen.
Andere wisselende activiteiten in
Kunsthuis **7X11** zijn tentoonstellingen
en kunstuitleen. Meer informatie op:
www.7X11.nl

7X BERT VAN OMMEN

PJ ROGGE- BAND

SUZE MAY SHO

ROMKE VAN DE KAA	TUINIEREN IN DE BEBOUWDE KOM	20 APRIL
LEZING		AANVANG 19ᵉ UUR

10 september 2005
20.30 — 24.00 uur
Festival met Film /
Video / Muziek

Patrijsplantsoen
Ypenburg, Den Haag
info: www.7X11.nl
toegang gratis

Video
Jeroen Kooings, Boszay Nemerofsky,
Robert Hamilton, TRAKTOR, Michel
Gondry, Nicolas Provost, Guido van
der Werve, Jan van Nuenen e.a.

Film
Psycho (Hitchcock 1960 /
Gus van Sant 1998)

Muziek
Eric et Chris

CLOSE ENCOUNTERS YPENBURG 2

This piece uses a single spot color printing onto colored
paper to achieve strong, bold results. Tints of the single
color can add depth and push the boundaries of what
monotone printing can achieve.

MOVIE FESTIVAL POSTERS

DESIGN
CATALOGTREE

CLIENT
CLOSE ENCOUNTERS

SPECIFICATIONS
- ➔ Rolitho paper
- ➔ Screen printing
- ➔ Single spot color

Close Encounters Ypenburg is an annual movie festival held on the streets of a suburb in The Hague, Netherlands. Catalogtree enjoyed producing its larger-format screen-printed posters. As a production technique, screen print is both restrictive and rewarding at the same time: loss in detail is counterbalanced by vibrant color. For the festival program, Catalogtree used rolitho paper, which is quite transparent and coated on one side. When folded into a program, the alternation of shiny and matte paper together with the see-through typography gave depth to the design.

124

TOUR FLYERS

DESIGN	CLIENT
IWANTDESIGN	**SOUND TRANSMITTER**

SPECIFICATIONS
- 45gsm newsprint
- Single spot color

Iwantdesign created two tour flyers, which were A3 (297 × 420mm/11¾ × 16½in) folded down to A5 (148 × 210mm/5¾ × 8¼in), to promote Sound Transmitter, contemporary music artists from Scandinavia. It chose to use newsprint (45gsm newsprint from Robert Horne Group) as it felt that its fragile quality would offset the powerful nature of the illustrations. John Gilsenan recalls, "Pioneer Print was a great help. Newsprint is tricky to print as it is so fine and can break up. We tried not to saturate the page with too much color and to keep it simple—hence each run was single color. It then had to run the press very slowly, and the same again with the folding machine.

"The project was a quick turnaround with a low budget—we worked on one idea each and chose the newsprint because it is a cheap way to achieve something that looks and feels quality."

Printing in a single spot color matched to a color swatch can yield simple, but striking results, as these posters clearly show. Brighter, bolder colors can be achieved using ready-mixed spot colors rather than four-color process colors.

ECO WORKBOOKS

DESIGN
CAROLYN GAVIN

CLIENT
ECOJOT

SPECIFICATIONS
- 100 percent recycled post-consumer waste FSC-certified, acid-free, chlorine-free
- Vegetable-based inks
- Vegetable-based glues

High environmental standards are an essential aspect of Ecojot's philosophy, whose portfolio of paper-based products boasts an exceptional level of detail in terms of its environmental credentials. These highly attractive workbooks are not only made from 100 percent post-consumer waste and printed using vegetable-based inks, but the paper is FSC certified, acid free and processed chlorine free. While these characteristics alone create a product range boasting exceptional environmental qualities, the company has sought further improvements by sourcing the materials from a supplier with similar environmental concerns. The paper mill is fuelled by biogas, a clean and affordable energy source, tapped from a nearby landfill site, thereby providing a viable use for an otherwise redundant and potentially polluting byproduct of the landfill process. Not content to consider the environmental characteristics of these workbooks alone, the company uses post-consumer waste in all secondary packaging and corporate labeling, and donates a portion of their profits to environmental charities.

The combined use of graphic patterns and flat color on the back and lower half of the front of these workbooks produces a smart, distinctive, and visually appealing finish, augmented and contrasted by the tactile surface of the covers caused by the use of 100 percent post-consumer waste.

ECO FILE FOLDERS

DESIGN	CLIENT
CAROLYN GAVIN	**ECOJOT**

SPECIFICATIONS
- 100 percent recycled post-consumer waste, FSC-certified, acid-free, chlorine-free
- Vegetable-based inks
- Vegetable-based glues

The range of file folders is manufactured from 100 percent post-consumer waste and printed using vegetable-based inks, providing admirable environmental attributes. The vibrancy of the inks is augmented by the excellent graphic design, which exploits the colors to their maximum effect. All materials are sourced and printed locally to minimize transportation costs, and suppliers are chosen based on their environmental credentials. These include the choice of paper mill, which not only supplies the paper stock, but is also fuelled entirely from biogas sourced from landfill sites.

Although such decisions are seldom seen as the responsibility of the designer, they are essential in extending environmental concerns beyond the product in isolation, and serve to support attempts by other industries to improve their environmental footprint. This commendable philosophy is evidenced in the company's decision to donate a portion of their profits to environmental charities, proving that environmental concerns not only make good sense, but make good business too.

The restrained use of typography to depict simple environmental messages discreetly is a well-considered detail that helps to underline further the inherent environmental credentials of this product range.

ECO SKETCHBOOKS

DESIGN	CLIENT
CAROLYN GAVIN	**ECOJOT**

SPECIFICATIONS

- ● 100 percent recycled post-consumer waste, FSC-certified, acid-free, chlorine-free
- ● Vegetable-based inks
- ● Vegetable-based glues
- ● Uncoated metal

This visually exhilarating range of sketchbooks firmly debunks the myth that environmentally friendly inks do not possess the same vivacity as those containing chemical enhancers that might be environmentally damaging. The entire range is printed using vegetable-based inks, manipulated expertly through a series of different designs to suit a variety of tastes. Vibrant, clean colors contrast well with the sensuous tactility of the paperboard of the covers, whose coarse surfaces result from being made from 100 percent unfinished post-consumer waste.

The choice of colors, tones, typography, and patterns across the product range produces a coherent identity for this environmentally-conscious Canadian brand, whose message aims to penetrate every aspect of the product range. Glues used in the lamination of inks to the paperboard are vegetable-based, and so biodegrade along with the inks and base material. The paper for the internal pages is not only made entirely from post-consumer waste, but is also FSC-certified as well as acid-free and processed chlorine free. Even the environmental impact of the spiral binding has been considered, by using only uncoated metal which allows it to biodegrade naturally or to be recycled without producing any harmful byproducts.

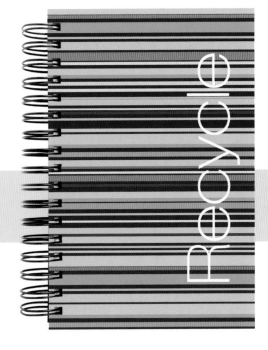

GREETINGS CARDS

DESIGN
HEIDE HACKWORTH

CLIENT
EARTH GREETINGS

SPECIFICATIONS
➔ Vegetable-based inks
➔ Resa 100 percent post-consumer recycled paper

Globally, the greetings card industry is huge and continues to grow rapidly, generating enormous quantities of waste as the card becomes an increasingly popular form of acknowledging or expressing sentiments across all manner of cultures. This entire range of cards is produced using 100 percent recycled paper stock and, with its stunning designs, does not compromise on quality when compared with virgin papers. In fact, the natural flecks and texture that 100 percent recycled papers can offer actually augments and enhances the environmental message of this brand.

This natural appearance is carried through to the envelopes, which are also made from unbleached 100 percent recycled paper, and which poses a delightful unpretentiousness and purity in their finish.

The strength of this brand message is conveyed powerfully in the charming designs, themselves inspired by natural themes. Each one serves as a little work of art, and the wide range of rich colors, vibrant tones, and gorgeous arrangements are all reproduced using vegetable-based inks, reducing their environmental impact.

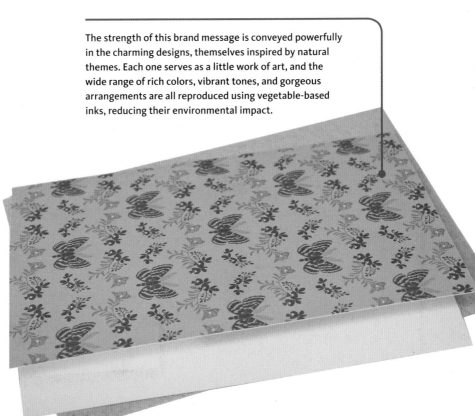

Every year 99,000 tons of dry waste is used to manufacture this particular brand of paper, preventing thousands of tons of virgin material entering the paper industry and thereby making a significant contribution toward safeguarding natural environments and biodiversity.

STANDARD PRINTING // VEGETABLE-BASED INKS

130 GIFT WRAP

DESIGN
HEIDE HACKWORTH

CLIENT
EARTH GREETINGS

SPECIFICATIONS
➔ Vegetable-based inks
➔ Resa 100 percent post-consumer recycled paper

The pleasure of wrapping a gift for someone special, or being the lucky recipient of a present, need not be compromised by imposing an unnecessary impact on the environment. A wide range of environmentally friendly gift wrap is available at a reasonable price, and the more designers and suppliers engage in providing customers with environmentally friendly alternatives, the more unacceptable it will become for others to produce gift wrap made of plastic or virgin paper. Environmentally friendly alternatives need not be bland or dull, as this stunning range of gift wrap proves. The designs draw inspiration from the natural environment and strongly evoke the Arts and Crafts traditions that so respected a balance between nature and work. So compelling are the designs that they could just as easily pass for wallpaper, and are works of art in themselves.

The printing is carried out at Finsbury Green, Australia's first carbon neutral printer, on paper manufactured in Denmark by one of the world's leading eco-friendly paper manufacturers.

PERMASET AQUA INK

DESIGN
LUKE BEST; CONWAY AND YOUNG; DAVID SHRIGLEY; MULTIPLE DESIGN AGENCY

CLIENT
I DRESS MYSELF; COLORMAKER INDUSTRIES

SPECIFICATIONS
- Screen printed by hand using water-based textile ink containing no white spirit

Making a positive difference by reducing the environmental impact of well-established commercial practices requires not only considerable dedication, but also a strong collaborative relationship with key business partners that share similar passions and objectives. This example demonstrates one such relationship where a commitment from both the textile printer and the ink manufacturer has led to a rapid increase in the commercial success of each. The product that has enabled these remarkable achievements is a water-based textile ink called Permaset Aqua. Developed and distributed by one of Australia's leading paint manufacturers, this innovation has the potential to revolutionize the way fabric printers can reduce their impact on the environment.

Most inks used by commercial screen printers contain plastisol to make them easy to use and perform well. However, plastisol inks contain PVC and phthalates that are harmful to the environment and have been linked to numerous medical disorders, and also require the use of harmful solvents in the cleaning process. In contrast, water-based inks do not contain PVC or phthalates and require only water, not solvents, to clean the screens down after they have been used. Furthermore, Permaset Aqua is entirely free of toxic chemicals and, unlike many water-based inks on the market, does not even contain white spirit. This ink has passed the highest level of international textiles testing and certification, which means it is safe to use on garments that come in contact with skin. The ink is highly durable to wash, rub, and dry-clean, is soft to touch, and has an intense pigment color for excellent coverage, opacity, and color brightness.

While creating such high-performance environmental products is an exceptionally demanding challenge in its own right, such products need to be promoted, developed, and sold to make them commercially viable, and commercial success requires collaboration with industry partners. This is where the establishment of commercial networks and partnerships proves vitally important, as demonstrated in this case study. The manufacturer of this ink provides it free of charge to a leading ecologically motivated and award-winning screen printer. This relationship facilitates an active and invaluable form of market research and assists in ongoing research and development. A complete range of colors, including metallic and fluorescent, ensures that the client's creativity is unrestricted while also respecting the environment.

133

SPECIALIST PRINTING

KUNSTENCENTRUM BELGIE POSTERS

DESIGN
SOUND IN MOTION

CLIENT
KUNSTENCENTRUM BELGIE

SPECIFICATIONS
- Coarse brown wrapping paper
- White silk paper
- 3D printing

Sound in Motion was commissioned by Kunstencentrum Belgie, an arts center in Belgium located in a building once used for importing and distributing colonial goods. "Distribution" was its inspiration for the 2005 arts festival; it used brown wrapping paper and labels with metallic colors to create contrast.

For the 2006 festival, designer Cools Pascal changed direction by creating a 3D poster design. This involved Pascal wearing 3D glasses throughout the creation of the project.

3D printing is a complex process that is difficult to get right. The background layer has to be oversized, layers that will be on similar depth planes grouped together, and different combinations of the animation layers must be exported to create the viewing angles. Special rounding effects can also be added for extra realism. Only then is the work ready to print as a 3D animation.

With these posters an interesting effect has been created by mixing a coarse brown wrapping paper with a strong white silk paper, which is printed and glued directly to the backing paper.

SILAS MARDER GALLERY PROMOTIONAL POSTCARDS

DESIGN/CLIENT
SILAS MARDER GALLERY

SPECIFICATIONS
➔ 15 × 22cm (6 × 8³/₄in) 100 percent PCW paper printed on Igen3 digital press
➔ Vegetable/soy-based inks

HORSE SHOW
AUGUST 26 - SEPTEMBER 25

SHED SHOW
THREE-DAY EXHIBITION
FRIDAY, AUGUST 25, NOON - 5 PM
SATURDAY, AUGUST 26, 10 AM - 9 PM
SUNDAY, AUGUST 27, 10 AM - 4 PM

PRINT SHOW
AUGUST 26 - SEPTEMBER 25

Printing promotional materials for one-off occasions, such as exhibitions and special events, demands specific consideration from designers and printers intent on maintaining high environmental standards. For limited print runs (under approximately 1,000 units), digital printing is the most cost-efficient, but vegetable- or soy-based inks cannot be used on these printing presses. Environmentally preferable inks can only be used on offset presses, thus causing an increase in the print run, which in turn raises the possibility of producing large amounts of waste paper. Printing small-batch jobs requires the careful consideration of, and compromise between, various factors such as the size of print run, the choice of inks, and the type of paper used. Further complicating these decisions are considerations such as the necessary production of printing plates for offset printing, which also require cleaning with chemical agents.

These important considerations are often confronted by this art gallery and leading environmental printer, whose productive relationship has led to a range of different solutions for the promotional material related to various exhibitions held at the gallery. Generally, when the print run is appropriately high, an Igen3 press is used with vegetable- or soy-based inks, and for smaller runs a digital press employing non-toxic inks is the process of choice.

TITTERINGTON'S SCONES LABELS

DESIGN
SHEAFF DORMAN PURINS

CLIENT
TITTERINGTON'S

SPECIFICATIONS
- ⮕ Eight-color flexography
- ⮕ Clear lamination
- ⮕ Die-cutting

Sheaff Dorman Purins used complex eight-color flexography to print labels for Titterington's Scones. Four-color process inks, plus four PANTONE specials, build up an elaborate color palette for these labels and help to reinforce the mildly eccentric "folklore" brand image established by the style and content of the illustration and traditional serif typography. Post-printing, labels were laminated and die-cut into a triangular shape, adding two finishing processes to the already extravagant print specification for this job.

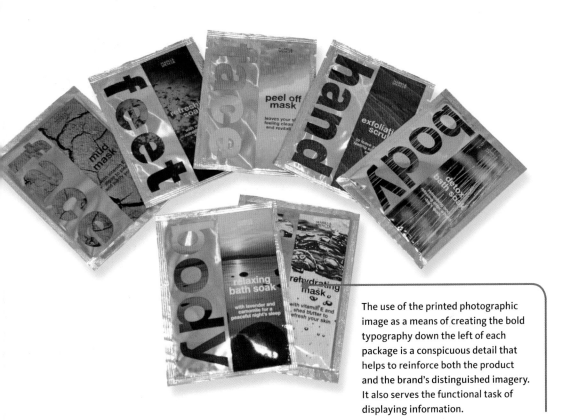

The use of the printed photographic image as a means of creating the bold typography down the left of each package is a conspicuous detail that helps to reinforce both the product and the brand's distinguished imagery. It also serves the functional task of displaying information.

TRAVEL TOILETRIES SACHETS

DESIGN
FLIPFLOP DESIGN LTD.

CLIENT
MARKS & SPENCER

SPECIFICATIONS
- Aluminum foil sachets
- Offset/flexographic printing

Packaging materials often have exceptional finishes in their own right and therefore can be used to augment alternative applied finishes. This range of products demonstrates the effective and impressive complementary use of the packaging material and a printing finish to create a charismatic appearance for an entire brand. Aluminum foil provides the base for each of the packages; its satin, light gray sheen projects a clinical, crisp, and superior tone that contrasts strongly and deliberately with the vivid colors of the photographic images. The high-quality reproduction of these images is essential to the effective outcome of the overall design. Each image has been carefully selected to reflect the nature of the product so that consumers can guess the contents of each sachet from the photograph through the associations it evokes.

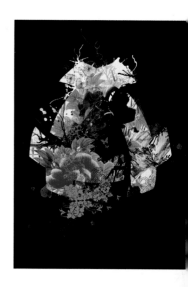

ASCOT SHOES BOXES

142

DESIGN
STUDIO OUTPUT

CLIENT
ASCOT SHOES

SPECIFICATIONS
- Four-color process
- High-gloss varnish
- Die-cutting

Studio Output designed this range of stackable boxes as a point-of-purchase piece for Ascot Shoes' Bamboo A. Each box was printed in full color, with an overall high-gloss varnish applied. The combination of vivid color, large areas of black, and (most importantly) this highly shiny, varnished surface, gives the viewer an impression of contemporary luxury with an oriental twist—the intention of the varnish is to recall the style of the intricate, oriental lacquered boxes. Post-printing, the flat form of each box was die-cut out of board.

CAFFÉ ARTIGIANO COFFEE LABELS

DESIGN
SUBPLOT DESIGN INC.

CLIENT
CAFFÉ ARTIGIANO

SPECIFICATIONS
➔ Coffee bags: four-color process, matte varnish, foil bags
➔ Labels: four-color lithography

Family-owned Caffè Artigiano produces and markets 16 varieties of artisan coffee, each of which is individually labeled with a full-color label design. The labels feature a selection of family photographs, each telling a different story. Although originally black-and-white, each image is printed in full color to provide a quality that reflects the age and character of old, treasured photos. Labels could easily have been printed using three special colors, but the print quality of photographic imagery would have been severely compromised, so four-color litho was selected.

Bags are also printed in four-color, then finished with a coating of matte varnish in order to provide a pleasingly smooth, tactile surface.

143

OIKO HANDMADE HEMP TEXTILES

DESIGN
OIKO (KATHY STEFANAC)

CLIENT
OIKO

SPECIFICATIONS
- Hand painted hot wax on hand-woven hemp
- Leather

Made from hemp, this range is sourced from Laos, Vietnam, and Thailand, and manufactured using a traditional method that has endured for centuries. These products provide an invaluable outlet for craft traditions at a fair market price, which contributes to the economic sustainability of the communities in this region. The raw fiber is processed into yarn by hand, and then woven on traditional looms by women from the Hmong ethnic group, before being dyed by a family-run business in Thailand. Owing to the nature and characteristics of hemp, the textured finish of each bag is subtly different depending on the quality of the woven material and the thickness of the fiber. This also impacts on how the natural dyes appear on the fabric. The shade of each finished product can vary depending on the quality of the woven hemp, and how it draws and retains the dye, giving each individual piece its own inimitable quality, which in turn helps to augment the exclusive character of the product range. This natural characteristic gives the product a unique quality that cannot be matched by synthetic fibers and denies a rigid standardization of materials and colors, which is one of the key attributes of this wonderfully rich and diverse collection.

The designs of this range of bags, which are applied using a hot wax method, demonstrate a fusion of contemporary Australian design and traditional handicraft techniques. They are inspired by Australian flora, such as the botanical gumnut print motivated by the stunning blossom of the Australian gum tree.

Leather, another natural material traditionally used by the Hmong people, has been introduced into this range of bags, and is used in the straps and zips. This helps to provide a dash of exclusivity and a sensuous variation in the textured finish of the product, compared with the woven hemp fiber.

Having gone to so much effort to process the hemp, manufacture the cloth, and apply the designs using hot wax, it is sensible from a commercial perspective to consider the range of applications suitable for this uniquely printed material. These cushion covers and wallets are just two of the many products which, through their sale internationally, help to support and sustain the lifestyles of those who manufacture these materials.

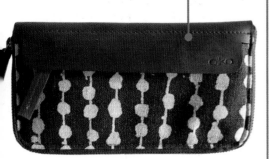

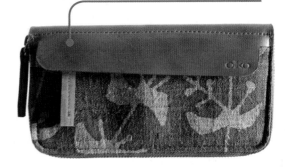

Many of the images for this Rinzen-designed point of purchase have cleverly used black backgrounds with centrally located areas of bright, vibrant color and white. This means that when back-illuminated, the light for the most part is blocked out by the dark areas and mainly shines through the brightly colored areas of organically shaped images, taking the viewer's attention away from the regular rectangular format of the display system.

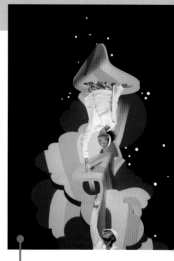

PUMA SIGNAGE

DESIGN
RINZEN

CLIENT
PUMA

SPECIFICATIONS
➔ Large-scale digital output

Puma Stores have in-store display systems to
take each new season's giant, digitally output,
point-of-purchase imagery. Some images are
presented with rear illumination, having first
been printed onto specialist translucent film.
Others simply slide into framing devices, after
being printed onto high-quality laser paper.
Large digital prints are an extremely cost-
effective way of producing large-scale, limited-
edition print runs, as images can be printed
straight from artwork without the need for the
costly platemaking necessary for lithographic
printing. In addition, there are fewer restrictions
on final print size, as digital printing presses
come in a great range of sizes, and shorter print
runs mean that, if necessary, prints can be tiled
together or trimmed to achieve any desired size.

147

LEVI'S. LADY STYLE

禁 断 の 果 実
いけないこと、してみたい。

LEVI'S. LADY STYLE

禁 断 の 果 実
いけないこと、してみたい。

LEVI'S POINT OF PURCHASE

DESIGN
VAULT49/BBDO

CLIENT
LEVI'S

SPECIFICATIONS
➔ Full-color laser printing

Levi's point-of-purchase designs by Vault49 and BBDO are evocative of stained-glass windows with biblical themes. These large-scale, dramatic images lend themselves well to specialist high-quality laser printing on translucent film, enabling the detail of the image to be seen while at the same time allowing bright white light to flood through and help to saturate colors.

These three designs are crammed full of tantalizing visual language, relating to Eve the temptress, provocatively wearing Levi's in her twenty-first-century Garden of Eden. The contemporary version of a stained-glass window, produced as a laser print, can only help to reinforce these erotic messages.

149

NIKE MADDIE POINT OF PURCHASE

DESIGN
VAULT49/CINCO

CLIENT
NIKE

SPECIFICATIONS
➡ Four-color laser printing

These two point-of-purchase panels for Nike were produced using high-quality, large-scale laser prints on translucent film. This allows rear illumination to enliven and enrich the colorful effect of energetic imagery, while adding a slightly reflective pearlescent quality to skin tones.

150

PLANT-DYED CLOTH

DESIGN/CLIENT
INDIA FLINT

SPECIFICATIONS
➲ Printing process using natural dyes on natural materials

Founded in 1999 and continually being improved and updated, the "Ecoprint" technique is a water-based printing process used to apply color to cloth. The inspiration came from a conviction that renewable natural plant dyes are not only viable alternatives to synthetic dyes, but also have a unique quality and intrinsic value in linking art and science.

　　The Ecoprint technique uses relatively small quantities of plant material in a recycled dye-bath and requires no adjunct mordants when protein fibers, such as silk or wool, are used. This reduces the quantity of resources needed to create the required dye as well as eliminating the need for other potentially toxic ingredients in the dyeing process. Like so many environmentally inspired techniques, Ecoprinting goes much further than simply producing a commercially practicable product in harmony with the environment—it encourages a complete reappraisal of the way in which the environment is perceived, understood, and disclosed by those that engage with the product.

All the dyes used in the range of Ecoprints are sourced from the Australin bush, which also serves as an inspiration for the astonishingly rich range of designs and colors.

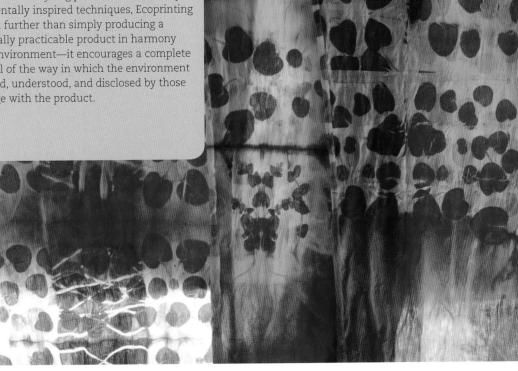

BIRKS JEWELERS CARRIER BAGS

DESIGN	CLIENT
PAPRIKA	**BIRKS JEWELERS**

SPECIFICATIONS
➔ Two-color lithography
➔ Foil blocking
➔ Lamination
➔ Metal eyelets

Paprika requested two new PANTONE colors specifically for Birks' use. "Using bespoke colors gave the bag a high-end finish and sense of uniqueness," comments creative director Louis Gagnon.

The custom blends were derived by mixing existing PANTONE shades to create special new colors. These were printed in full strength to bleed across the outside and the inside of these bags, epitomizing the luxurious nature of the brand.

To reinforce the seductive nature of these bags, Paprika also used various high-quality finishing processes, including foil blocking, lamination, and the inclusion of matching-colored metal eyelets that hold in ribbon and cord handles neatly.

MBG & SDS RECORD SLEEVE

DESIGN
ZION GRAPHICS

CLIENT
MBG & SDS

SPECIFICATIONS
➲ Two-color lithography including silver

Zion Graphics designed a number of labeling devices for MBG & SDS. This disc has a two-color label, expertly printed in silver and pink. Zion also used die-cut holes in the outer sleeve, positioned to ensure that the interior album labeling plays a vital role in the exterior sleeve image. Stuck to the top right-hand corner of this sleeve is a two-color adhesive label, providing a platform for record details.

This is an interesting and cost-effective alternative to printing directly onto the sleeve and, by using the same colors as on the record, this outer label unifies the entire design.

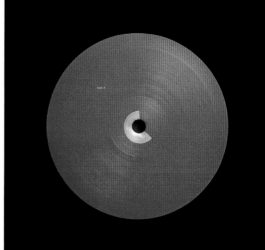

SPENDRUPS WINES LABELS

DESIGN
ZION GRAPHICS

CLIENT
SPENDRUPS VIN

SPECIFICATIONS
➲ Two-color lithography including one metallic color

The labeling for Nygårda is printed simply in two-color litho, however, one of the PANTONE colors is metallic. Both sets of labels feature black plus the same special metallic color.

The level of sparkle and reflectivity produced by PANTONE metallic inks used in litho printing is generally not as great as what can be achieved with the use of foil blocking, but it is a much more cost-effective process. Different results can be achieved by careful selection of paper stock, and printing metallics onto coated paper or board produces some of the most metallic-looking results with this ink. However, selecting uncoated, absorbent material creates a very different, more subdued effect. Varnishing areas printed with PANTONE metallic inks can also enhance the sparkle.

155

ELIZABETH ARDEN SPA MATCH HAIRCARE

DESIGN
ALEXANDER ISLEY INC.

CLIENT
ELIZABETH ARDEN

SPECIFICATIONS
- ➔ Bags: offset printing, gloss varnish, die-cutting
- ➔ Bottles: silkscreen printing, custom-mixed pearlescent colors

156

For this range of bags and labels the designers used specialist pearlescent inks. "The unusual shimmering properties of these colors were selected to reflect and reinforce the actual product effects and benefits," comments Lisa Scroggins of Alexander Isley.

we've got
your
perfect
match.

match hair care by Tricoci
available throughout the U.S. at
Red Door Spas, Mario Tricoci Salons
+ selected department stores

TRICOCI

match

The bags were printed in matching colors using offset litho. In order to create a similar surface shimmer and sheen, the design was gloss-varnished, and the finished print was die-cut and creased to form its final shape. A contrasting white cotton handle references the product color that features so prominently in the labeling.

The labeling on these pots and bottles was directly screen printed onto the surface, creating an ultra-smooth, pleasingly tactile result, reminiscent of the product's effect on skin. The containers are translucent, so the product itself plays an important role in the overall color palette of the labeling.

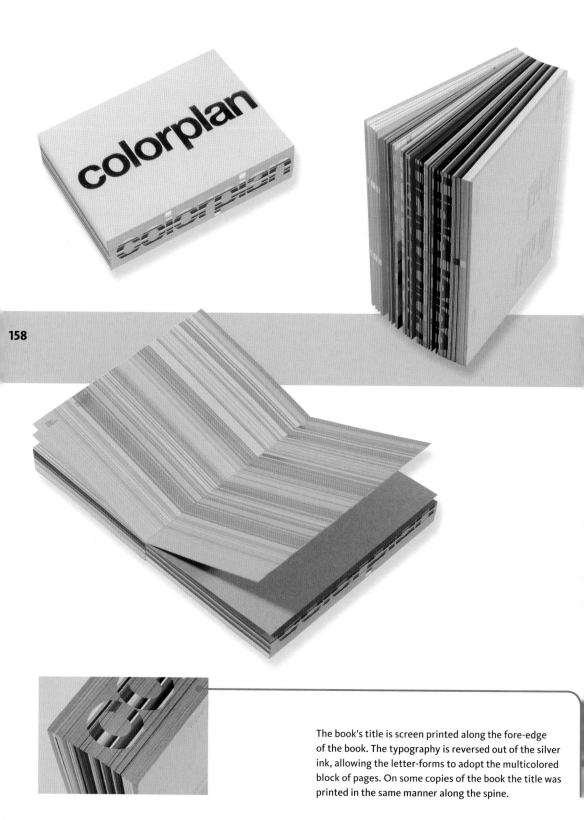

The book's title is screen printed along the fore-edge of the book. The typography is reversed out of the silver ink, allowing the letter-forms to adopt the multicolored block of pages. On some copies of the book the title was printed in the same manner along the spine.

COLORPLAN BOOK

DESIGN
SEA DESIGN

CLIENT
GF SMITH

SPECIFICATIONS
● Four-color process with specials and UV varnish foil blocked
● Die-cut
● Perfect-bound with bookbinders' cloth

This small, solid block of a paper-sample book shows the full range of colors, weights, and embossed finishes available in the range. The designers show examples of a wide variety of printing techniques and effects that can be used on the stock, including one-, two-, three-, and four-color process lithography, special colors including metallics and fluorescents, foil blocking, UV varnishes, die-cutting, and embossing. The fore-edge of the book is screen printed in silver, with the paper's names reversed out, revealing the vast spectrum of colors available in the range.

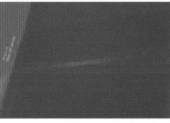

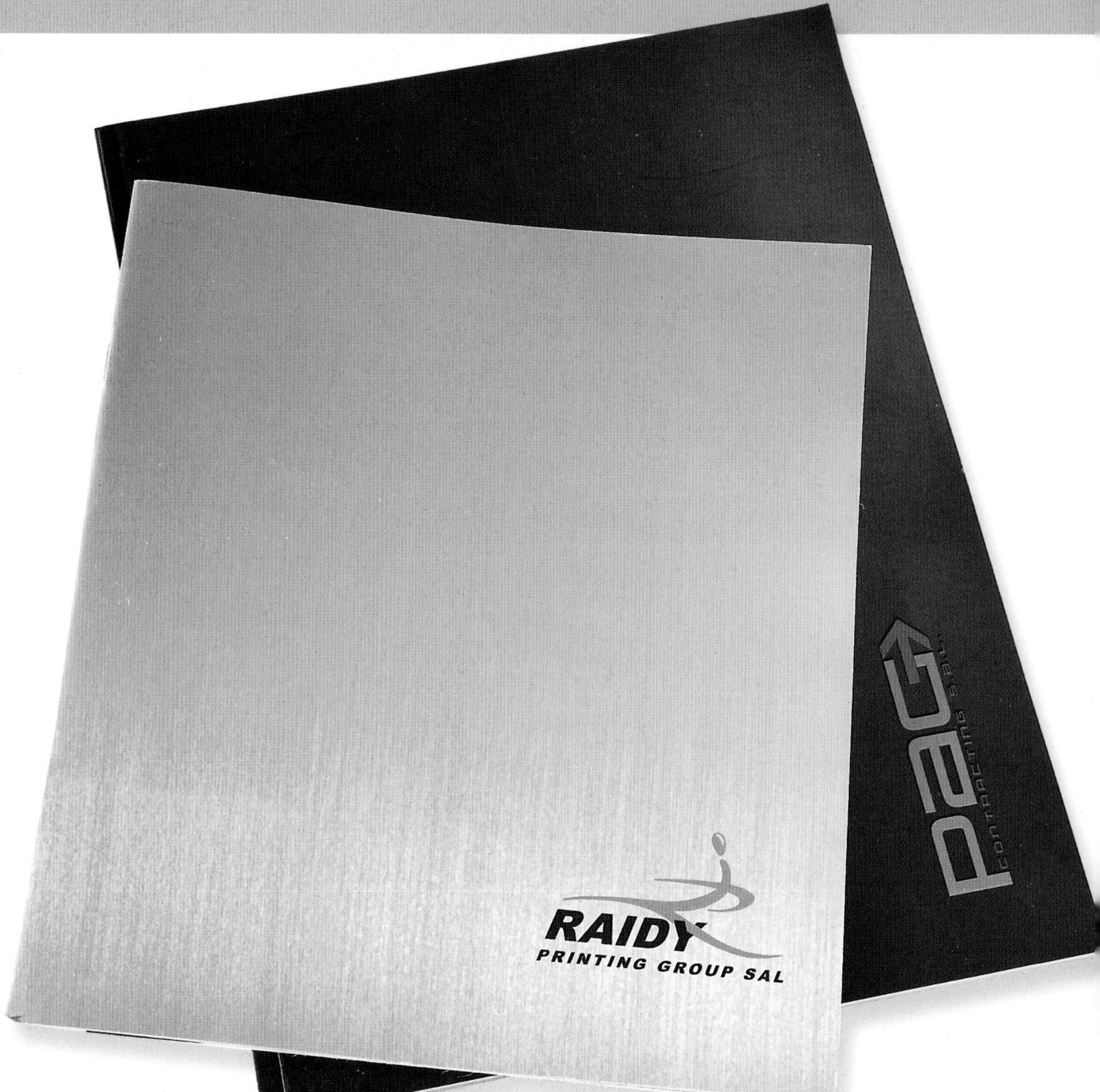
RAIDY
PRINTING GROUP SAL
CONTRACTING S.A.L.

CORPORATE BROCHURES

DESIGN
RAIDY PRINTING GROUP

CLIENT
RAIDY PRINTING GROUP AND P.A.G. CONTRACTING

SPECIFICATIONS
- Five-color process (four colors plus MetalFX printing technology)
- Virgin paper that conforms to the Chain of Custody standard
- Water-based coating

Metallic finishes have long been seen as a printing finish fundamentally incompatible with the objectives of the environmentally conscious designer, because among their ingredients are chemicals and metallic particles that potentially harm the environment. Also, their application requires a separate pass in the printing process for each metallic ink, thereby increasing set-up costs as well as causing a corresponding increase in the quantity of resources this demands. Consequently, they are rarely used on environmental printing jobs and eco-friendly clients seeking the sparkling or dazzling effects that metallic inks provide have simply had to make do without.

However, these brochures, which boast a highly metallic finish throughout, use only one extra ink, as opposed to separate spot colors for each metallic color, owing to a new printing technology called MetalFX. This allows a huge variety of metallic colors to be produced from a single application of silver or gold ink beneath the standard four-color (CMYK) process. The MetalFX system relies on the transparent characteristics of the CMYK inks to allow the sub-layer of silver or gold to infuse the colors above with a shiny metallic appearance.

" With PAG, quality is never an accident; it is always the result of high intention, sincere effort, intelligent direction and skilful execution. "

161

LION CRIB SET

DESIGN/CLIENT
PIXEL ORGANICS

SPECIFICATIONS
- Organic cotton sateen
- Low-impact printing

Achieving extraordinary, quirky, or novel finishes is not always desirable. When the objective is to produce an environmentally sound product or finish, the greatest challenge might simply be to equal a conventional finish without causing harm to the environment. The use of organic cotton represents one such step. Conventional cotton farming comprises 3 percent of the world's total crop yield, yet it uses 25 percent of the world's chemicals for crops—it is swimming in chemicals. The organic cotton industry is therefore keen to promote a chemical-free alternative. This range of products uses organic cotton for children's clothing and bedding accessories. Essential to the quality of the product and the strength of the brand is the use of graphics and the way these are printed onto the cotton. A specially designed, low-impact printing process has been devised to deliver a high-quality and colorfast printed finish to the surface of the fabric in an infinite range of colors, eliminating the need for heavy metals and toxic runoff. Once applied, the ink is soft to touch and does not degrade the fabric, making it an ideal alternative to standard textile printing, which often relies on harmful chemical ingredients and high-impact processes.

ODDITY CARDS

DESIGN/CLIENT
DOTZERO DESIGN

SPECIFICATIONS
➡ Two-color silkscreen printing

To most designers, a heavyweight brown paper bag is an item of beauty evoking a bygone age of quality and attention to detail. Dotzero Design utilized them as a starting point for packaging their latest self-promotion, screen printing each bag with two colors. The inks have a distinct matte quality that forms a memorable contrast with the sheen of brown paper. This design makes effective use of the contrast by building color and sheen into the detail of retro illustration. Dotzero Design selected silkscreen as the method of printing, as the inks produce precise areas of quality, opaque color which would be impossible to achieve with any other printing method.

163

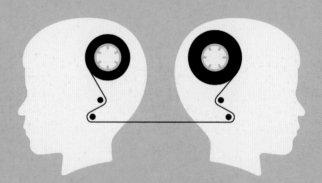

THE BOOKS

GREAT AMERICAN MUSIC HALL

W/ TODD REYNOLDS

04.23.07

THE SMALL STAKES POSTERS

DESIGN	CLIENT
THE SMALL STAKES	**VARIOUS**

SPECIFICATIONS
- Two-color silkscreen printing

Shown here are three fascinating examples of music gig posters. The Castanets poster was printed using two contrasting colors—dark brown and blue—on white stock. The poster is framed by images of overlapping leaves, printed using a coarse halftone screen to capture the tonal detail produced by light and shade.

The Books poster is printed on off-white paper with metallic silver and black inks. Screen printing metallic inks tends to give a more truly metallic, glistening effect than is possible to achieve with litho inks alone, although the end result is affected by the quality of paper used, and coated papers provide a smoother, harder surface that is likely to achieve the most noticeably metallic effect.

This Shins poster was printed with three opaque colors onto a minty green stock, which is significant as the ink used was specially selected to totally block out the color of the paper. This is a very useful property of screen printing, as it allows the designer to select a distinctive colored stock, and ensure that ink is going to sit on top of the selected material without being altered by it in any way.

165

PRODUCT PACKAGING

DESIGN	CLIENT
GREG BARBER CO.	**JURLIQUE**

SPECIFICATIONS
- ➔ Recycled egg crates
- ➔ 100 percent PCW paper
- ➔ Printed full-color using soy-based inks

Many companies now realize how important a responsible environmental policy is for their business and how this affects the loyalty of their customers. While this is true generally, it is particularly pertinent for companies engaged in businesses where health, well-being, and the environment play a central role. Product packaging is an essential platform for gaining customer loyalty, but also an equally effective tool for losing it, if designed and manufactured badly.

The range of excellent packaging for this famous brand of cosmetics reflects the company's stringent environmental and ethical standards by using only 100 percent recycled fiber and printing in brilliantly rich colors using soy-based inks. This has been achieved using concentric screening, an innovative form of AM screening using small, thin, concentric rings. The result is unparalleled detail, vibrant colors, and wider color gamut. It gives the appearance of continuous tone, because it controls the dot gain, allowing for higher line screen.

The customer is informed of the efforts that the company has made to produce environmentally responsible material by discreetly printing the various specifications relating to the printing and manufacturing on each package.

Biodynamic Beauty Collection

Jurlique Classics Collection

Rose Body Care Collection

Jurlique

Jurlique

Lavender Body Care Collection

The three screen printed plates are overprinted on different pages, creating even more complex abstract fragments of the coastlines and typography.

EXHIBITION GUIDE

DESIGN/CLIENT
HECTOR POTTIE

SPECIFICATIONS
- Screen printed cover in three colors
- Singer-sewn through

This book was produced to accompany an exhibition in Berlin that featured a series of screen printed maps focusing on the areas in which the designer grew up. The maps were produced as solid colors to draw attention to beautiful coastlines and lakes. The book uses the same screen printed maps, but overprinted to create rich, abstract patterns. These are complemented by another mapping process, by which the designer charted his location and interests over a five-year period. A variety of cover designs appear on different copies.

169

CADBURY FLAKE DARK PACKAGING

DESIGN
V4 STUDIO/CADBURY TREBOR BASSETT

CLIENT
CADBURY

SPECIFICATIONS
- "PMYK"
- White screen printing
- Metallic polyester 180 corrugate
- Die-cutting

"PMYK" as opposed to CMYK inks were specified by V4 Studio for this point-of-purchase design. The "P" in this case stands for Cadbury's signature color purple, and is present in place of cyan ink. By specifying a precise, specially mixed purple, V4 could ensure absolute corporate color consistency throughout every chocolate brand within Cadbury's extensive portfolio.

Metallic polyester plays a fascinating role within the visual language of this design. "The metallic substrate was used to mimic the bar wrapper and also to give the unit a premium and indulgent feel," comments Carol Meachem of V4 Studio.

HUNT'S MUSTARD AND KETCHUP LABELS

DESIGN
MATT GRAIF DESIGN

CLIENT
CONAGRA FOODS

SPECIFICATIONS
- Four-color web offset printing
- Die-cutting

Hunt's Mustard and Ketchup labels were printed in four-color process, but rather than using conventional litho, they were printed on a web-fed press. Sheet-fed presses only allow for single-sided printing. Web-fed presses, however, are fed from a continuous roll of paper, making double-sided printing possible. Web printing is also far quicker than conventional litho presses, and tends to be used when large quantities of items are required.

Post-printing, these designs were die-cut to create the slightly curved shape for wrapping around bottles.

FOLDING & BINDING

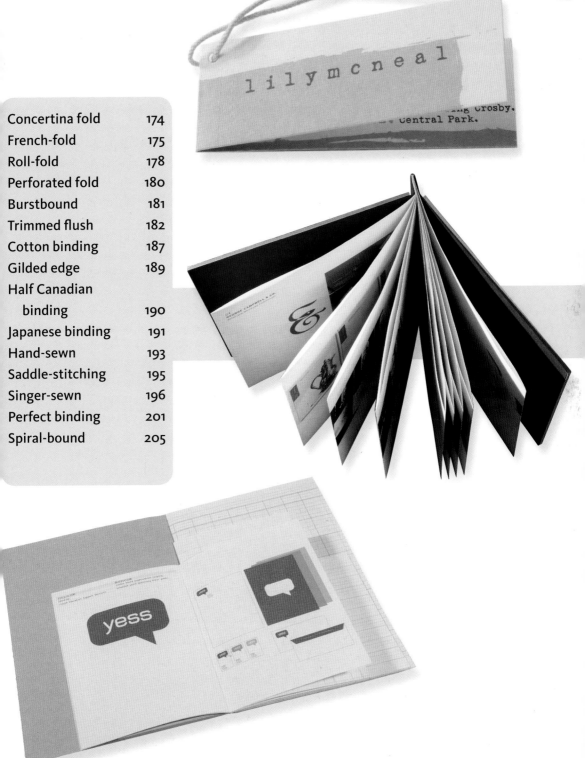

LAND SECURITIES QUARTERLY NEWSLETTER

DESIGN	CLIENT
RADFORD WALLIS	**LAND SECURITIES**

SPECIFICATIONS
- Incarda Silk 250gsm
- Die-cut
- Loose-leaf inserts
- Concertina folded

Property developer Land Securities produce quarterly newsletters to help keep the local community in touch with what is happening on their sites. The brief to Radford Wallis was to create a generic format that could be used for all their various developments. These newsletters were to be delivered direct to local residents, so they needed to be sealed in a self-containing way. The solution was to create a concertina that incorporated the masthead, held the reply card in place, and folded together to seal itself. Radford Wallis opted to use James McNaughton's Incarda Silk 240gsm with die-cut finishing.

174

Loose-leaf inserts were ingeniously held in place by die-cutting a tab from the back to marry up with die-cut slits throughout this concertina-folded document. Loose-leaf pages can be added as the tab punches through all the pages and out onto the front cover, holding everything together.

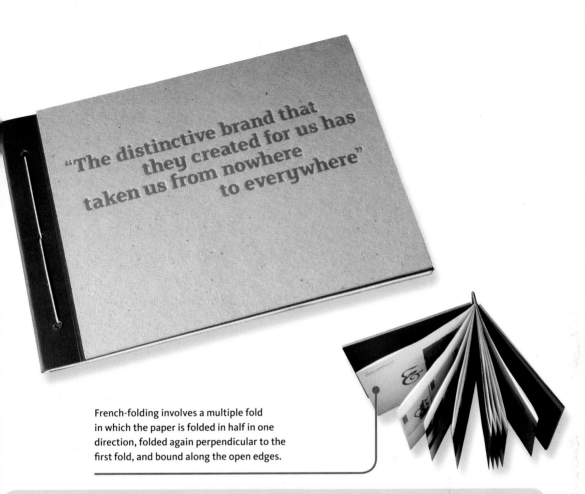

"The distinctive brand that they created for us has taken us from nowhere to everywhere"

French-folding involves a multiple fold in which the paper is folded in half in one direction, folded again perpendicular to the first fold, and bound along the open edges.

FOLDING & BINDING // FRENCH-FOLD

NEVIS DESIGN PROMOTIONAL BOOK

DESIGN/CLIENT
NEVIS DESIGN CONSULTANTS

SPECIFICATIONS
- Bedrock duplexed to Colorplan Cobalt
- Stab stitched
- Three-hole Singer-sewn
- Foil blocked
- 50gsm biblio
- French-folding
- 2,000 micron Bedrock for the cover

In this self-promotional piece for Edinburgh-based Nevis Design, the materials were chosen because of their diversity and contrast. Nevis experienced minor problems with the binding—it chose to try several different types of sewing and various treads to get the desired result. Any initial problems were solved through good collaboration with Beith Printing and the binders Hipwells.

Stock and finishing included Bedrock duplexed to Colorplan Cobalt, stab stitched, three-hole singer-sewn, and foil blocked. Text pages used 50gsm biblio finished with French-folding and the cover used 2,000 micron Bedrock.

TYPE SPECIMEN BOOK

DESIGN/CLIENT
UNDERWARE/PIET SCHREUDERS

SPECIFICATIONS
➲ 48 pages
➲ Cover printed four-color process plus specials
➲ Singer-sewn through

This type-specimen book goes beyond the realms of the standard four-page leaflet often sent out to announce a new font design. The name of the font, Sauna, is the starting point for this elaborate production. Printed on a special stock that is capable of withstanding temperatures of up to 120°C (248°F), some pages are printed with a special humidity-controlled ink that only becomes visible inside a sauna, where it reveals hidden messages. The covers are French-folded around a stiff sheet of card; this allows the same stock to be used throughout the book while giving the covers more stability.

The book is Singer-sewn through, a binding method that is incredibly strong and which, as it requires no glues, is able to withstand extreme temperature changes.

The covers are French-folded around a stiff sheet of card; this allows the same stock to be used throughout the book while giving the covers more stability. The book is Singer-sewn through, a binding method that is incredibly strong and which, as it requires no glues, is able to withstand extreme temperature changes.

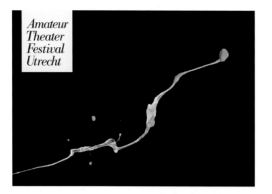

In roll-folding, the page is repeatedly folded, in panels or sections, from one edge toward the other. When folded out, this results in a number of "pages" being visible at the same time.

AMATEUR THEATER FESTIVAL POSTER AND FLYER

DESIGN
MAIN STUDIO

CLIENT
UTRECHT CENTRUM VOOR DE KUNSTEN

SPECIFICATIONS
- ➔ Posters
- ➔ Program booklet
- ➔ Leaflet
- ➔ T-shirts

Main Studio designed a poster and flyer for the Amateur Theater Festival in Utrecht, the Netherlands. Eggs were used as a metaphor for the reaction of crowds confronted with a bad performance. Eggs thrown at people were photographed to create strong, poetic images. The campaign, rolled out mainly around Utrecht, consisted of two posters (A1; 594 × 841mm/23½ × 33in), a program booklet (A5; 148 × 210mm/5¾ × 8¼in), a leaflet (A5; 148 × 210mm/5¾ × 8¼in), and T-shirts.

STUDIO LOCASO VISUAL DIARY

DESIGN/CLIENT
STUDIO LOCASO

SPECIFICATIONS
- CMYK and PMS 319
- 135gsm Sovereign offset
- Japanese binding
- White bubble-wrap envelope

Studio Locaso's Expressions is a visual diary that encourages people to get their hands dirty when it comes to design. Studio Locaso's aim was to express itself using a variety of design techniques and mediums, resulting in a beautifully presented, emotive, and evocative visual diary.

The diary was printed using CMYK and PMS 319 on 135gsm Sovereign offset. It contains gatefolds, roll-folds, and an overall varnish throughout. Its hard cover is white buckram with a Japanese binding and it was packaged in a white bubble-wrap envelope.

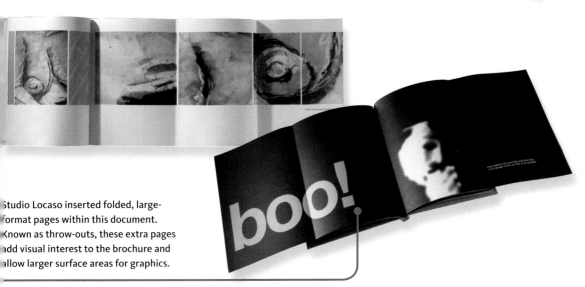

Studio Locaso inserted folded, large-format pages within this document. Known as throw-outs, these extra pages add visual interest to the brochure and allow larger surface areas for graphics.

LILY MCNEAL HANGTAGS

DESIGN
KBDA

CLIENT
LILY MCNEAL

SPECIFICATIONS
➔ Two-color lithography
➔ Scoring
➔ Perforation
➔ Woven fabric

These lily mcneal hangtags are printed in two PANTONE colors. What makes this design unusual is the fact that the light gray color is a special pastel PANTONE. PANTONE pastel shades give a light, flat, solid color, as opposed to being made up by a halftone screen. They are created by blending different percentages of certain PANTONE inks with varying amounts of extender to create a lightened tone of the original color combination.

These hangtags also use scoring and perforation to create a fold, plus textured detail that is reminiscent of actual stitching. Light gray has been purposefully selected and combined with a deep, rich, warm brown. This not only creates a subtle, natural effect that reinforces the softness of lily mcneal knitwear, but also echoes the need for gentle care of the garment

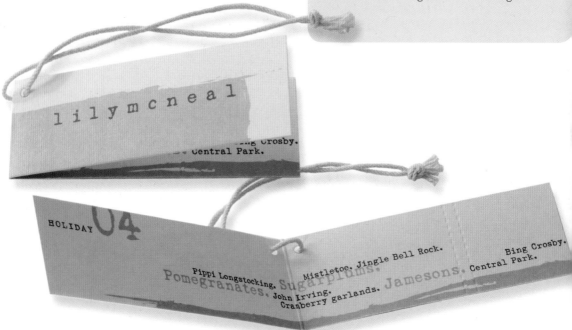

Fabric labels were woven in colors that match those chosen for print. It is interesting to view these labels from the rear as the type, although in reverse, still has surprisingly sharp detail, an effect which could also be utilized in a label design.

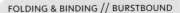

VILA NAIÁ-CORUMBAU PROMOTIONAL FOLDER

DESIGN
SUPERBACANA DESIGN

CLIENT
VILA NAIÁ-CORUMBAU

SPECIFICATIONS
- ➔ Handmade wooden box
- ➔ Cartão Cinza paper
- ➔ 120gsm Rives Tradition Pale Cream paper

Superbacana Design created this unique folder to publicize the Hotel-Pousada Vila Naiá-Corumbau in Bahia. It is packaged in a handmade white wooden box to profile the special ambience of the hotel. Materials used included Cartão Cinza paper for the cover and 120gsm Rives Tradition Pale Cream paper for the text pages.

181

With the burstbound method, sections of the book are glued rather than sewn in. While stronger than perfect binding, the resultant bind is not as strong as that achieved with thread-sewn sections.

TONY CRAGG EXHIBITION BOOK

DESIGN
MADETHOUGHT

CLIENT
CASS SCULPTURE FOUNDATION

SPECIFICATIONS
- 152 pages
- Casebound cover printed in one color, two colors, four-color process, and five colors
- Thread-sewn sections

Produced to accompany an exhibition of work by British sculptor Tony Cragg, this beautiful book follows the process of the construction and installation of sculptures as they are placed in the rural landscape. The first 48 pages are printed on a light weight of pale blue stock, and reproduce a photographic record of the sculptures' installation. The mono images are printed in a single color that changes from section, starting in a rich brown, then purple, and finishing in black. Next, the book dramatically switches to a heavy, silk-coated stock, exquisitely printed in four-color process and showing the sculptures in position. It then reverts to an uncoated white stock in a heavier weight to match that of the silk section. This section contains an essay, quotes, and a biography; the text sections are printed in black onto a pale yellow background, complemented by a series of color photographs of the artist in his studio and by images of the sculptures being constructed. The cover uses the same pale yellow background, with a landscape image of the park printed in full color, although the image has a misty quality that turns it almost monochromatic. The cover boards are trimmed flush to the text pages on the top and bottom edges, which gives the book a special quality.

KIENHOLZ ART CATALOG

DESIGN
SPIN

CLIENT
HAUNCH OF VENISON LONDON

SPECIFICATIONS
➔ 96 pages
➔ Printed four-color process plus one special
➔ Thread-sewn sections

Produced to accompany an exhibition the husband-and-wife artists held at the Haunch of Venison in London, this art catalog is fairly conventional in format, except that the cover boards have been trimmed flush to the text pages, which gives the book a solid, hard edge. The grayboards have a cool gray paper bonded to them; this wraps around the spine which adds to the clean lines of the cover. Warm gray is printed full bleed inside to divide sections, and is also used in the text pages.

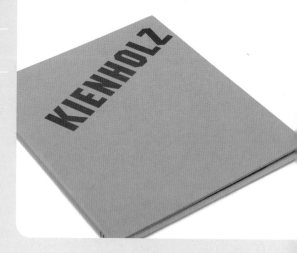

The grayboards have a cool gray paper bonded to them that wraps around the spine. The boards have been trimmed flush to the text pages, giving the book a solid, hard edge.

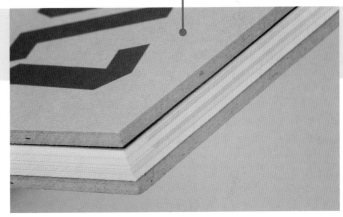

ANTI-SLAVERY INTERNATIONAL PROGRAM

DESIGN	CLIENT
INARIA	**ANTI-SLAVERY INTERNATIONAL**

SPECIFICATIONS
- Six colored posters
- Stenciled die-cut
- Brightly colored paper stock

Anti-Slavery is a charity working exclusively against slavery and related abuses. Its annual fund-raising ball is an essential part of its income. Each year its chosen theme ensures the seriousness of the message is well delivered. The theme "Colors of the World" inspired Inaria to produce a program that was relevant to the slave trade, while allowing a positive and relevant message by using color. Six different-colored posters, designed to decorate the walls of the event, also folded down to become dust jackets for the program itself. Distinctly colored sections within the brochure, stenciled die-cut typography on each of the divider pages, and brightly colored paper stocks were all used in tandem with real-life imagery to create a strong graphic language.

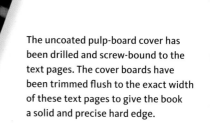

The uncoated pulp-board cover has been drilled and screw-bound to the text pages. The cover boards have been trimmed flush to the exact width of these text pages to give the book a solid and precise hard edge.

ETC SWINGTAGS

DESIGN	CLIENT
BRIGHT PINK	**ETC**
COMMUNICATIONS DESIGN	

SPECIFICATIONS
- Single- and four-color lithography
- Die-cutting
- Cotton binding
- Stitching

This range of swingtags for accessories brand etc was produced in both four-color and single-color print, and each tag has been die-cut to create an oversize hole that accommodates the tie. This cut-out is also an integral part of the design, and speaks to any potential purchaser of etc products' unconventional, contemporary approach to design. The tag uses both paper and fabric. Each tag has a bound edge that is covered with black cotton binding, and the mix of materials reflects and reinforces the unusual nature and design detailing of etc products.

187

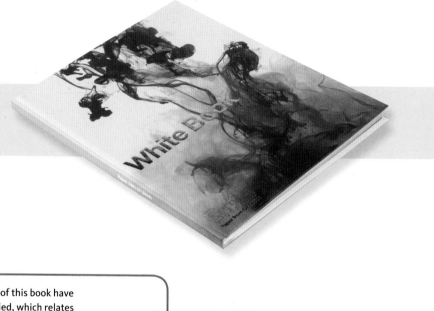

The trimmed edges of this book have a silver gilding applied, which relates to the silver foil blocking on the cover. This effect gives the brochure a very luxurious quality.

GF SMITH BOOK

DESIGN
SEA DESIGN

CLIENT
GF SMITH

SPECIFICATIONS
- 72 pages
- Casebound cover printed four-color process
- Foil blocked
- Edge foiled burstbound

Produced for the paper merchants GF Smith, this beautiful book is purely a platform to enable the various different paper stocks to shine. A series of exquisite photographs of colored ink in water, taken by photographer John Ross, are reproduced in full color on each page, and because each page is a different stock, the book becomes a rich, tactile experience. The final section is printed in one color only on a pale yellow stock and forms a visual record of the process of making the book. Both the cover and the endpaper at the front of the book are printed with silver foil blocking, which is picked up on the gilded edges of the book block.

JEFF LUKE CATALOG

DESIGN
SECONDARY MODERN

SPECIFICATIONS
- 48 pages plus six tabbed index dividers
- Four-page cover printed one color and four-color process
- Half Canadian bound

Featuring the work of the late Jeff Luke, this catalog has been sympathetically designed to reflect the style and ideas of the artist. It features six thumb-tabbed dividers printed in black on an uncoated buff card, and this—combined with the half Canadian binding—gives the catalog the appearance of a user's manual. The sections are printed on various stocks (uncoated; coated silk; and fibrous, uncoated gray), in black and four-color process.

The catalog is half Canadian bound, a process where the text pages are wire bound into the back of the cover, this allows the spine and front cover to remain clean with no visible signs of white.

To achieve the Japanese binding, holes were punched through the book near the spine and the pages stitched together. Any thread can be used for this binding method, from carpet thread to nylon thread, and even waxed dental floss. A length eight times the book's height is required.

HALLOWEEN PROMOTIONAL BOOK

DESIGN/CLIENT
ORANGEYOUGLAD

SPECIFICATIONS
- 44 pages
- Strathmore Writing paper
- Carnival Vellum cover
- White foil stamped
- Japanese binding

OrangeYouGlad collected scary stories from friends and family and compiled them into this nifty little Halloween promotional book. The *Little Bleak Book* serves and OrangeYouGlad's annual "thank you" to clients, contributors, vendors, consultants, and other associates. The 44-page book was printed on Strathmore Writing paper at a copy shop. The Carnival Vellum cover was white foil stamped and trimmed by Little Rhody Press. OrangeYouGlad used a Japanese binding technique to bind the books in-house.

EMMI'S PORTFOLIO

DESIGN/CLIENT
EMMI

SPECIFICATIONS
- 58 pages
- Four-page cover printed four-color process
- Thread-sewn sections

Created as a self-promotional piece for the designers, this brochure groups together a variety of samples of work, with each project shown at a different size and format from the next. Each project also has a sheet of preprinted ruled paper that is used as a divider wrap, and is produced at a different physical size. Each of the sections is thread-sewn into the card cover, using different-colored thread for each project.

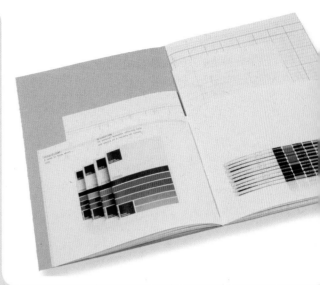

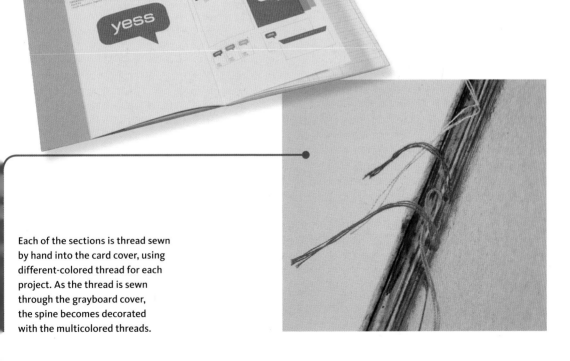

Each of the sections is thread sewn by hand into the card cover, using different-colored thread for each project. As the thread is sewn through the grayboard cover, the spine becomes decorated with the multicolored threads.

Saddle-stitching binding is achieved by applying staples through the centerfold of nested signatures. This is the most common form of binding.

J.LINDEBERG IDENTITY

DESIGN
SATURDAY

CLIENT
J.LINDEBERG

SPECIFICATIONS
➔ Saddle-stitching

Saturday created the identity for J.Lindeberg's sports label Future Sports. Based on a circle, the identity spans packaging, labeling, stores, and advertising. Today it can be seen on some of the world's best athletes in skiing and golf, two areas where J.Lindeberg has redefined style.

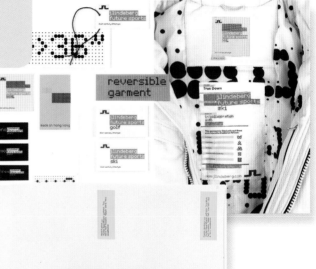

AMAT FINQUES BROCHURE

DESIGN	CLIENT
BASE DESIGN	**AMAT FINQUES**

SPECIFICATIONS
- 16 pages plus eight-page cover
- Printed four-color process and six colors
- Singer-sewn section
- Uncoated stock

Printed in Spanish, Portuguese, and English, this simple brochure for a Spanish estate agent works with three key colors to separate the languages: red, warm gray, and a tint of black. The brochure is printed on a soft, off-white, uncoated stock that prevents the clean typographic cover treatment from becoming too cold and hard. As a contrast to the understated cover, the inside front and back flaps are printed full bleed in a vibrant warm yellow. Inside, the colored typographic treatment is illustrated with a series of full-page images of selected key properties from the company's portfolio. The quality of the brochure is further enhanced by the binding technique, with red, Singer-sewn thread used as a more elegant alternative to the more conventional saddle-stitched option

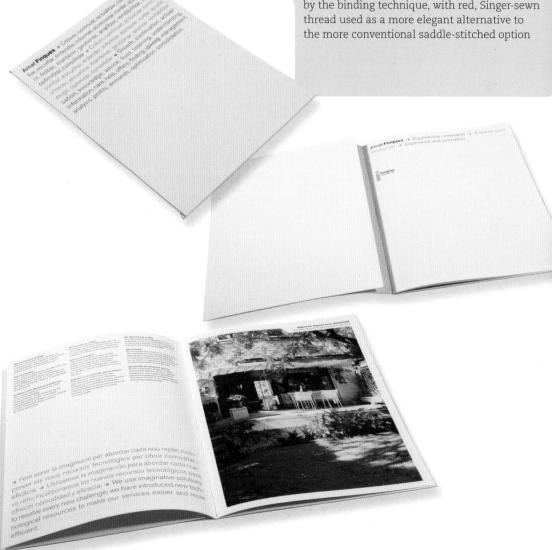

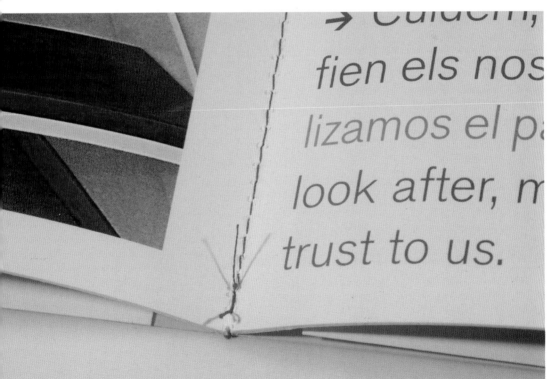

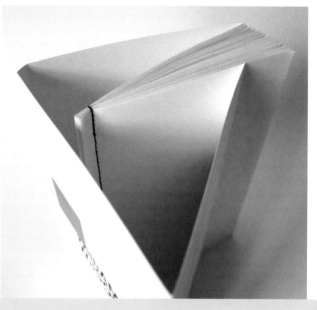

JORGE MACCHI
EXHIBITION CATALOG

DESIGN	CLIENT
BASE DESIGN	**LA CASA ENCENDIDA**

SPECIFICATIONS
- 96 pages
- Printed four-color process plus one special
- Singer-sewn through

This catalog was produced to accompany an exhibition of the work of Argentinian artist Jorge Macchi at La Casa Encendida in Spain. The exhibition was called Doppelgangers, and the catalog follows the same theme. The artist chose a story by Edgar Allan Poe, "William Wilson," and this story runs throughout the catalog in a fairly conventional manner. However, on closer inspection it is found that the French-folded pages can be unfolded to reveal a series of images by the artist. These images are mirrored on a central axis, echoing the idea of the Doppelganger. The catalog is Singer-sewn through and has a cover with a conventional spine applied.

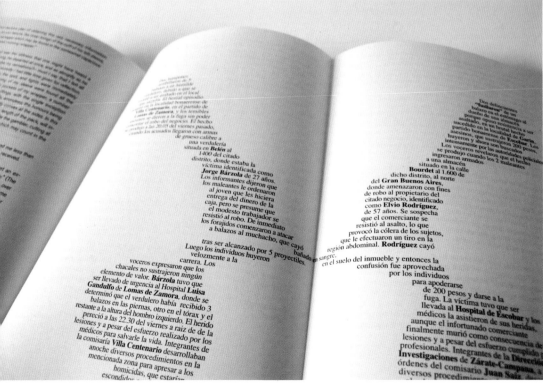

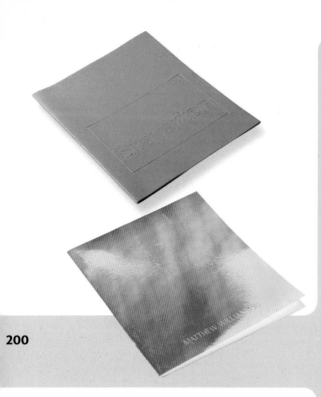

STAVERTON FURNITURE CATALOG

DESIGN	CLIENT
SEA DESIGN	**STAVERTON**

SPECIFICATIONS
- 24 pages plus four-page cover
- Printed four-color process
- UV varnish
- Heat welded
- Singer-sewn section

This text-light brochure for a London-based office furniture manufacturer conveys all the information required through beautifully clean photography and high production values. Every page of the brochure is printed with a full-bleed UV gloss varnish, which evokes the quality and high production values of the furniture.

The brochure is Singer-sewn, whereby an industrial sewing machine is used to bind it; a line of matching yellow thread runs down the central crease, forming a very strong binding. The brochure's cover is made from a soft, flexible PVC, with the company's logo heat-welded onto the front. The cover is bonded to the first and last pages of the brochure, thereby hiding the thread on the spine. It becomes seamless with the text pages, because the color match of PVC yellow and litho-printed yellow are spot on.

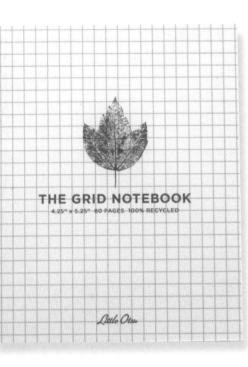

THE GRID NOTEBOOK
4.25" x 5.25" 80 PAGES 100% RECYCLED

Little Otsu

GRID NOTEBOOK

DESIGN
**JASON MUNN; JEREMY
CROWN; YVONNE CHENE**

CLIENT
LITTLE OTSU

SPECIFICATIONS
➔ Offset printing with soy-based inks
➔ 100 percent post-consumer recycled paper
➔ Bound using animal-free adhesives

Designed to be an iconic notebook decorated entirely with grids throughout, this eye-catching product uses outward appearance and materials to elevate its perceived value and raise it above the heaving crowd of notebooks available on the market. The minimalist design and cover art provide a charismatic appearance, while keeping the quantity of ink used to a minimum. Manufactured from 100 percent post-consumer waste, this notebook also and thereby helps to support recycling. Soy-based inks have been applied throughout, with two colors used for the covers and one color for the grids on the internal leaves. No synthetic coatings have been used, so the product's finish remains characteristically natural, while also allowing it to be recycled, or to biodegrade more efficiently.

The spine of the notebook has been perfect bound using animal-free adhesives.

The perfect-bound document is wrapped in a cover made from 300gsm uncoated stock with a textured and tactile finish that both reflects the purity of the materials from which the brochure is made and the ecological character of the products within.

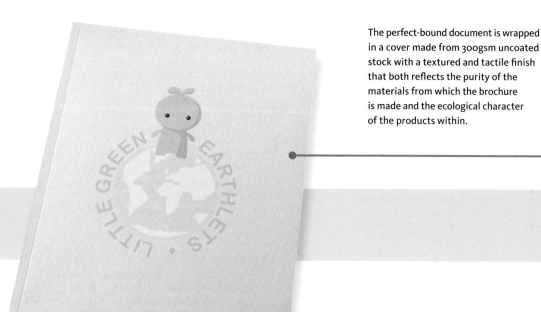

The accompanying marketing material uses the same weight of uncoated paper and the same natural color range as the cover of the product catalog to produce a strong and coherent brand image that reflects robustly the company's ecological principles.

EARTHLETS PRODUCT CATALOG AND MARKETING MATERIAL

DESIGN
PEEKABOO DESIGN

CLIENT
LITTLE GREEN EARTHLETS

SPECIFICATIONS
- Four-color process using vegetable-based inks
- FSC-certified chlorine-free paper
- Cover—300gsm
- Internal pages—110gsm
- Printed on Challenger offset press powered using only renewable energy

Sustainable issues are rarely so starkly in the spotlight than when framed within the context of baby products. Unlike in many industry sectors aimed at adult consumers, organic, ecological, natural, and non-toxic are bywords that represent the rule and not an exception to it. This retailer of baby products maintains this uncompromisingly high standard across its entire product range, so when it came to designing and producing a new product catalog and supporting marketing material, it was essential that this ethos was reflected throughout.

The objective from the outset was to produce a highly desirable document that would sit proudly on a coffee table or anywhere in the home and not be thrown straight in the bin. Printed in natural colors throughout using vegetable-based inks on FSC-certified paper, the compact 105-page catalog, brimming with excellent environmentally friendly ideas and products, appears delightfully cheerful, tidy, and fresh.

An invitation to receive the Little Green Earthlets catalogue...

Here at Little Green Earthlets we have been very busy over the summer finding lots of exciting new stuff for you, your baby and your home. Our new bigger and better than ever brochure has a fab look and we just can't wait to share it with you.

You'll find a beautiful range of super-stylish organic baby and toddler clothing and accessories for day and night, simply stunning toys that'll make you want to be a child again and quirky home accessories made from all manner of recycled bits and bobs. You'll also find those can't do without baby essentials from Mother-ease washable nappies (we have the biggest range all in one place) and eco-disposables from Moltex & Wiona to high chairs and natural cot mattresses.

* To celebrate we are offering Mother & Baby readers 10% off their first order with us. Simply mention this code ZXSCX58 (offer ends 15 Jan 2008) when you place your order online, by phone or by post.

If you would like to receive a copy of the new Little Green Earthlets brochure simply tear off and fill in the form opposite with your name and address and return it to us. We'll then send you our brochure – we're sure you are going to love it. Can't wait for the brochure ? - then go to www.earthlets.co.uk and browse online.

We hope to hear from you very soon.

the earthlets team

* Yippee!
10% off your
first order

I would love to receive a copy of the new Earthlets brochure

Name
Address
Postcode
Email

If you would like to receive our email newsletter please tick here

We don't share details off - anyone else so feel assured you won't receive random mailings from other companies

MB58

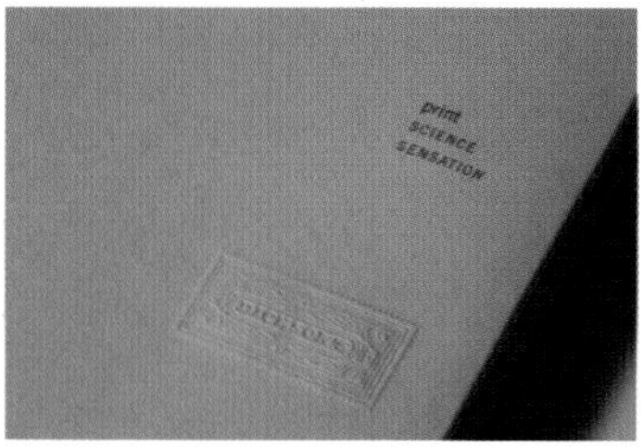
SCIENCE
SENSATION

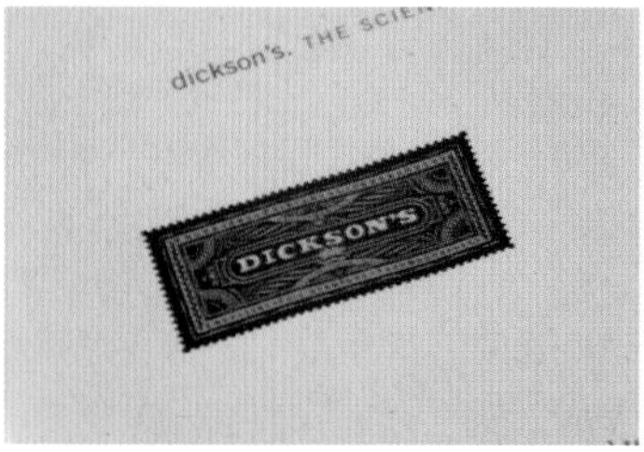
DICKSON'S

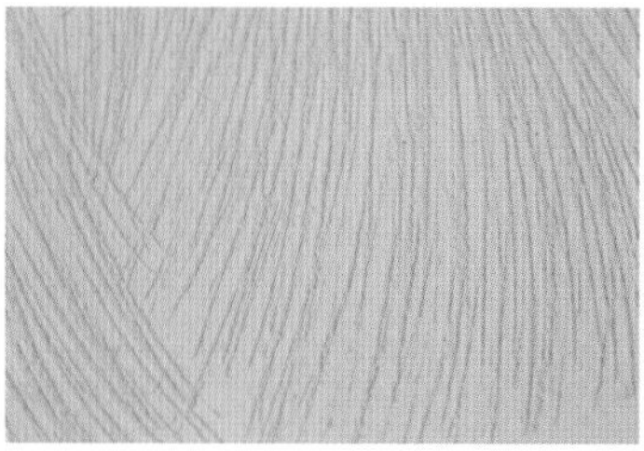

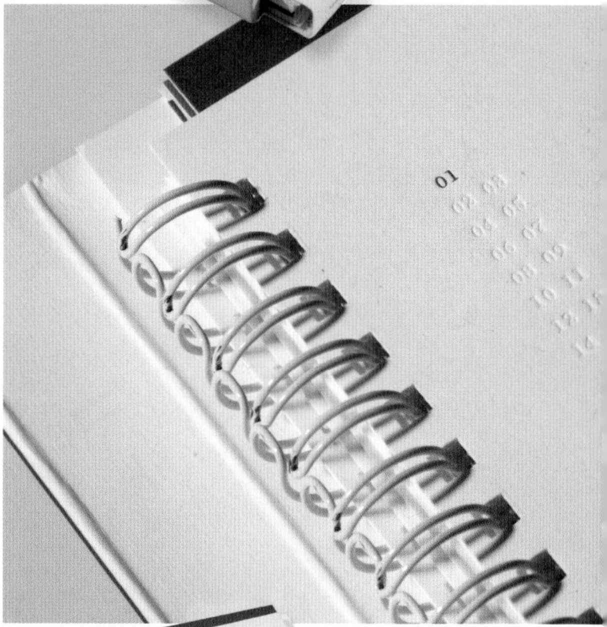
01

PRINT COMPANY BROCHURE

DESIGN
PH.D

CLIENT
DICKSON'S PRINTING

SPECIFICATIONS
- 16 pages plus inserts
- Cover printed four-color process
- Letterpress printed
- Thermographed
- Embossed
- Debossed
- Engraved
- Foil blocked
- Die-cut
- Perforated
- Scored and drilled
- Spiral bound

The Science of Sensation was designed to visually illustrate every aspect of print production available from this Atlanta-based print company. Housed within a sturdy slipcase, the full Canadian-bound brochure sits with its spine protruding by 25mm (1in). Each of the 16 pages is French-folded, with the bottom edge sealed to form a pocket. These pockets contain cards which elaborate upon the one-line questions posed on the outside of the page.

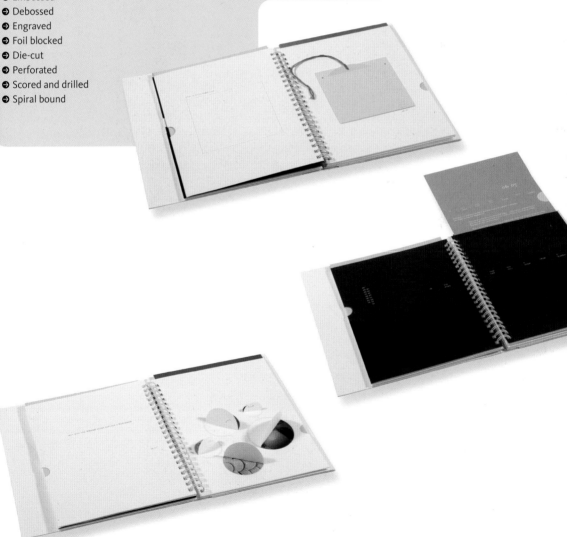

FINISHING

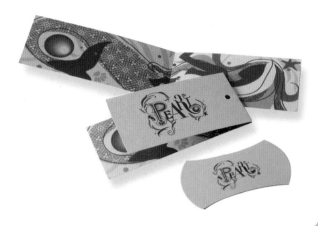

PEARL BAGS, HANGTAGS, AND BUSINESS CARDS

DESIGN
IE DESIGN + COMMUNICATIONS

CLIENT
PEARL

SPECIFICATIONS
- Two-color lithography
- Die-cutting
- Embossing

Two PMS colors were printed independently, and overprinting each other in order to give the effect of three colors within the decorative namestyle of "Pearl." One of the PMS colors is also printed in an all-over complementary pattern on the inside of the hangtag. Pearlescent stock was selected to highlight the name of the store, a cutting form was used to create the distinctive shape of the business card, and the circle in the swash of the "R" was embossed.

ETC SWINGTAGS

DESIGN	CLIENT
BRIGHT PINK	**ETC**
COMMUNICATION DESIGN	

SPECIFICATIONS
- Four-color laser printing
- Die-cutting
- Hand-folding

Designed to label etc products' more prestigious and traditionally inspired creations, these swingtags were laser-printed in a variety of colorways, die-cut, then carefully assembled. As with many elaborate tag designs, the tag has become as much a part of the highly desirable purchase as the actual product. In the case of these miniature dolls, the wide variety of colors, combined with the hand-finishing, ensures that every doll is a unique, one-off piece that adds considerable value to the purchase.

209

FULLY LOADED TEA BOXES AND DISPLAY

DESIGN
SUBPLOT DESIGN INC.

CLIENT
FULLY LOADED TEA

SPECIFICATIONS
- Tea boxes: five-color lithography, sealing varnish, die-cutting
- Display: bent, frosted Plexiglas, single-color screen printing
- Flavor menu: clear plastic frame

Subplot Design Inc. used a number of interesting finishing processes to create point-of-purchase material for fully loaded tea. Boxes containing individual flavors were printed in five-color litho and finished with die-cutting to create the unique drop-down drawer for restaurant and café display purposes. This bespoke method of presentation is an attractive alternative to the familiar ripped box front.

Individual tea boxes are grouped in sixes for display within a specially created Plexiglas point-of-purchase container. The Plexiglas has been cut, screen printed, and specially heated along fold lines to allow for the formation of folds.

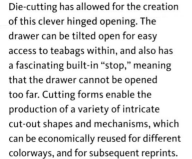

Die-cutting has allowed for the creation of this clever hinged opening. The drawer can be tilted open for easy access to teabags within, and also has a fascinating built-in "stop," meaning that the drawer cannot be opened too far. Cutting forms enable the production of a variety of intricate cut-out shapes and mechanisms, which can be economically reused for different colorways, and for subsequent reprints.

212

MAPLEX SWATCH HANGTAG

DESIGN
MSLK

CLIENT
MAPLEX

SPECIFICATIONS
➔ Four-color process using vegetable-based inks
➔ Die-cutting

Maplex is an environmentally conscious company, and therefore wanted to find a way of getting its product samples into the hands of architects and designers in a sustainable manner. To accomplish this, MSLK designed a swatch in the form of a swingtag that cleverly uses the materials left over from die-cutting the brochure cover. It is attached to the wiro binding of the Maplex brochure, with a metal-ball-link chain in a way that ensures both maximum impact and stand-out quality on architects' shelves.

This entire project was printed in four-color process, but uses environmentally friendly vegetable-based inks. All materials and processes were utilized in a manner that reflects and reinforces the company's contemporary, ethical approach.

ACORN CONCEPTUAL TEXTILES IDENTITY

DESIGN
STUDIO OUTPUT

CLIENT
ACORN CONCEPTUAL TEXTILES

SPECIFICATIONS
➔ Die-cuts
➔ UV laminates

Studio Output's identity for Acorn, a conceptual textiles house that creates swatches for high-end fashion labels, was based on its interpretation of the word "acorn." Utilizing drawn tree elements, the logo was combined with varying textured and patterned backdrops to create a juxtaposition of form and tone. These elements were changed seasonally in Acorn's catalogs to represent the changes in color, texture, and materials used in the collection. Die-cuts and UV laminates on the business cards and presentation folders further enhanced the decorative and tactile qualities of the designs.

ROMANTIQUE
A transitional large scale floral and leaf tapestry

BATH HOUSE PAISLEY ROSE LABELS AND TAGS

DESIGN/CLIENT
BATH HOUSE

SPECIFICATIONS
- Two- and four-color lithography
- Textured paper
- Ribbon
- Braid

The tags for these two products utilize an appealing interplay between a number of different materials and the complex manner in which they are brought together at the finishing stage. Ribbon, braid, coated and uncoated papers, and textured and smooth papers combine within single tags, folded tags, self-adhesive labels, and a wraparound label (all using the same color palette) to form a cohesive and distinctive style.

215

The floral paisley pattern of this wraparound label is printed on uncoated, textured stock, and is complemented by a blue-and-white polka-dot hangtag on another uncoated, textured stock. The effect is completed by a perfectly matching blue silky ribbon, neatly knotted to hold the hangtag in place. Such detailed hand-finishing reflects on the products themselves and suggests they are to be used for self-indulgence.

GAVIN MARTIN ASSOCIATES DIRECT MAILER

DESIGN	CLIENT
NB: STUDIO	**GAVIN MARTIN ASSOCIATES**

SPECIFICATIONS
➔ GF Smith 320gsm Accent Antique Archival card
➔ Printed in Black and Cool Grey 8

Printer Gavin Martin Associates asked NB: Studio to design a direct mailer to announce its move to new offices in the Tea Building in Shoreditch, London. Inspired by its new location, NB:Studio decided lavishly to letterpress the typography on GF Smith card and then painstakingly hand stain all 1,000 cards with a tea ring to reflect the idea of removal men leaving tea stains all over the office.

The A6 (105 × 148mm/4 × 5⅜in) finished mailer was printed black and Cool Grey 8 on 320gsm Accent Antique Archival by GF Smith. The tea stains were printed by hand with real tea substituting CMYK with Earl Grey, Darjeeling, Rooibos, and English Breakfast teas.

Nick Clark design has a habit of producing fantastic and highly desirable designs that can only be finished by hand. This project is no exception, requiring tearing, burning with a blowtorch, and hand-folding.

ROYAL BANK OF SCOTLAND INVITATIONS

DESIGN	CLIENT
NICK CLARK	**ROYAL BANK OF SCOTLAND**

SPECIFICATIONS

- 20 percent cotton, acid-free calcium carbonate buffered stock
- Blowtorch
- Hot wax seals
- Large bread knife
- Unfragranced hair spray

This invitation not only involved using a 20 percent cotton, acid-free calcium carbonate buffered stock (160gsm Canaletto Grossa from R. K. Burt), but also a blowtorch, hot wax seals, a large bread knife, and unfragranced extra-strength hair spray from L'Oréal. Once printed, each invitation was hand-torn to give a rough edge, slashed on the sides with a bread knife, severely scorched with a lit blowtorch, then put out, carefully dusted down, and sealed from excessive smudging using odorless hair spray. The invitations were then hand-folded into an old-fashioned self-envelope and given a hot wax seal with a brass seal and tartan ribbon. To achieve a further level of "sinisterness," they were inserted into a tissue-lined, gusseted envelope made by a small family business in London.

217

HONEY B TOYS

DESIGN
LAURA VARSKY

CLIENT
GARY LO

SPECIFICATIONS
➔ Marker pen

Laura Varsky was commissioned by Gary Lo to help promote his range of toys. The resulting point-of-purchase designs were produced by hand, using nothing more complicated than a few marker pens. Working directly onto the plastic "creatures," Laura selected gold and black permanent marker pens to ensure durability of design. This method of production provides the opportunity for a great deal of design flexibility, and also means that each finished character is totally individual.

BUZZIN' FLY CD PACKAGING

DESIGN
IWANT DESIGN

CLIENT
BUZZIN' FLY

SPECIFICATIONS
- ➤ Six-page digipak
- ➤ Heavyweight board and bespoke blue tray
- ➤ Matte blue foil
- ➤ Block throughout

Iwant Design has been responsible for developing artwork for Buzzin' Fly Records since the label's 2003 inception. The agency designed the label's fly logo and font which, initially inspired by Pablo Ferro, has since taken on an identity all of its own. Taking layers of typography and graphic elements, the agency worked to create manic layers of color across the reverse board. For this release the budget was limited, but the agency stretched the processes where possible. This included the incorporation of a bespoke blue tray, designed to complement the blue foil blocking used throughout, and with indents replicating the diagonal cross used throughout the design.

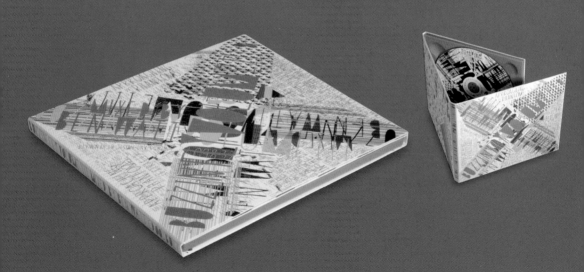

The agency has used matte blue foil blocking throughout the design to pick out elements such as the title and the musician's name. The color contrasts well with the reverse board and plays with the slight embossing inherent in foil blocking to create another level and texture within the design.

PREŠERNOVO AND POZVAČIN WINE LABELS

DESIGN
KROG, LJUBLJANA, SLOVENIA

SPECIFICATIONS
- Four-color lithography
- Gold foil blocking

These wine labels make use of "branded" laid stock. For the Prešernovo wine, the designer chose to have the grain of the paper, and therefore the watermarking, running vertically down the label, thus accentuating the height of the bottle.

The labels are printed in four-color litho, highlighted with carefully positioned gold foil blocking. This finishing process, combined with the use of specialist paper, creates a sense of exclusivity and high quality as well as long-standing repute.

This stunning invitation uses several
techniques in its finishing. Perhaps the
most interesting, yet understated, is the
use of a black foil blocking on black card,
with fantastic results.

ABU DHABI TOURISM AUTHORITY INVITATION

DESIGN	CLIENT
FOUR IV	**ABU DHABI TOURISM AUTHORITY**

SPECIFICATIONS
- Gloss UV
- Black foil
- Gold foil
- GF Smith 135gsm and 540gsm Colorplan

This invitation was designed by London's Four
IV for the Abu Dhabi Tourism Authority for the
opening of its UK office. The invitation was printed
using gloss UV, black foil, and gold foil on GF
Smith's 135gsm and 540gsm Colorplan Ebony.

The label on the lid of A New Baby soap and sponge is an unusual cross between a hangtag, with white-and-green stripy ribbon threaded through a hole at the top edge, and an adhesive label. It looks like a hangtag, but is affixed to the box with two sticky pads that raise it slightly above the surface. Interesting and well-designed hangtags generally denote style, and the effect of this concept is to suggest that this is a "designer" product.

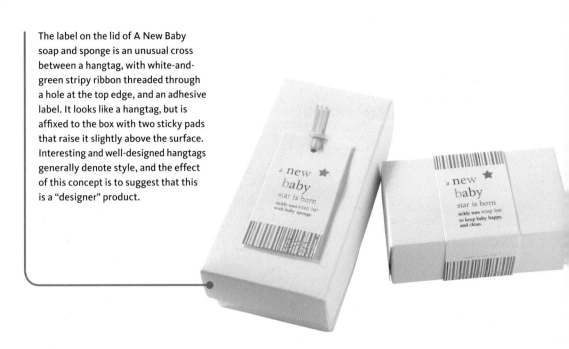

BATH HOUSE A NEW BABY LABELS

DESIGN/CLIENT
BATH HOUSE

SPECIFICATIONS
- Four-color lithography
- Silver foil blocking
- Uncoated stock
- Ribbon

Labeling for the A New Baby range from Bath House employs complementary fresh colors out of the four-color set, high-gloss silver foil blocking, and a matte surface of white uncoated stock. It also demonstrates a superb quality of silver foil blocking as an integral part of the design.

225

The silver foil blocking on this hangtag highlights the pleasing contrast of gloss and matte surfaces, and exemplifies the ability of the process to reproduce fine and very tiny lettering.

EMI MUSIC PUBLISHING "IMAGINE"

DESIGN	CLIENT
AIRSIDE	**EMI**

SPECIFICATIONS
- Embossing
- Art paper

Airside has created a range of point-of-purchase posters to promote the sales of classic music reissues, including this poster for "Imagine." This design uses only one carefully selected and beautifully executed finishing process: embossing. It is very uncommon to see such large areas of embossing; this process is more usually selected to highlight small areas of focused detail. Here, Airside bravely commissioned an extensive area of embossing in order to subtly highlight and reinforce the meaning of the lyrics.

IMAGINE
THERE'S NO COUNTRIES
IT ISN'T HARD TO DO
NOTHING TO KILL OR DIE FOR
AND NO RELIGION TOO
IMAGINE
ALL THE PEOPLE
LIVING LIFE IN PEACE
YOU MAY SAY THAT I'M A
DREAMER
BUT I'M NOT
THE ONLY ONE
HOPE SOMEDAY YOU'LL JOIN US
AND THE WORLD
WILL LIVE AS ONE

Airside specified plain, light-colored art paper to highlight the effect of embossing. The edge of each letterform is crisp and appears slightly raised next to the perfectly flat, sunken area created by the die. Overall, this large point-of-purchase poster is an appropriately gentle way of highlighting the meaning of John Lennon's famous lyrics.

Embossing of the brand logo helps it to subtly rise from the silver surface of the container—enough to be noticeable, but not so much as to undermine the uncluttered visual composition of the overall design.

228 MICHAEL'S COOKIES GIFT BOX

DESIGN
FUELHAUS

CLIENT
MICHAEL'S COOKIES

SPECIFICATIONS
- Arjowiggins Curious Metallics paper stock
- Metallic ink
- Four-color process
- Spot colors
- Embossing

A complete visual makeover transformed what was originally a white cartonboard container into this distinctive package, which boasts a range of printing and production finishes employed to reflect the premium character of the product. The printing effects include spot metallic and PMS (Pantone Matching System) inks applied to silver paper stock. The parallel lines of color contrast strongly with the silver base and are reflected in the detailing on the container's lid, which is printed four-color process. Spot UV varnishes in a speckled pattern on the silver surfaces provide an element of visual detailing intended to echo the character of the product's uneven surface.

Two passes of the same PANTONE color can be used to enrich and intensify the final result, ensuring that the deepest, flattest shades have been achieved. In this instance, two passes of black have been used to give a truly opaque effect, which is reinforced by a coat of matte varnish.

FINISHING // EMBOSSING

RED KNOT WINE LABELS

DESIGN
**KENDALL ROSS BRAND
DEVELOPMENT AND DESIGN**

CLIENT
RED KNOT WINE

SPECIFICATIONS
- Two-color lithography
- Matte and gloss varnish
- Embossing

Kendall Ross has used a combination of specialist printing and finishing processes to achieve the design vision for luxury wine brand Red Knot.

"The unique, hand-drawn knot has been printed in a PANTONE red, which has been set against a background created from two passes of black ink, creating an extra-rich effect. Areas of gloss and matte varnish were applied to reinforce the luxurious nature of this product and, combined with embossing, result in a pleasing tactile quality," comments designer David Kendall.

230

FERNANDO DE CASTILLA SHERRY BOTTLES

DESIGN
DESIGN BRIDGE

CLIENT
FERNANDO DE CASTILLA

SPECIFICATIONS
- Embossing
- Four-color process plus three specials
- Gold foil
- Textured self-adhesive paper

Labeling is often the designer's best, and sometimes only, opportunity to present the appropriate character for a product packaged in glass bottles, as the high costs incurred by bespoke production mean that many products are packaged in generic bottles. This heightens the role of good label design and, budget permitting, choice of closure in delivering the distinctive branding or product characteristics. The design of the labels in this range has captured the eminent character of this high-quality brand by using a distinctive tactile paper with deep-embossed details. The nature of the paper evokes the distinguished quality of handmade papers, with their mottled and uneven surfaces. This refined character is reinforced by the elaborate embossed fonts that dominate the center of the label. The soft shade with which they have been printed has the subtle distinction of a watermark, though the drop shadow provides a visual clue that the motif stands proud of the label's surface. The product title at the base of the label has been printed in black at the smallest readable font size so as not to undermine the overall delicate appearance.

OLOROSO
JEREZ XERES SHERRY

FINO
JEREZ XERES SHERRY

Matte laminating involves bonding a matte plastic film directly to a sheet of paper using heat and pressure. Laminating protects the printed sheet and prevents the "cracking" that can occur where large areas of solid inks are printed across folds.

HELLO DUUDLE BOOK PROJECT

DESIGN
**HELLO DUUDLE,
WIGGLETON PRESS**

CLIENT
HELLO DUUDLE

SPECIFICATIONS
- 600gsm grayboard coated with 128gsm art paper
- Matte laminated
- Gold foil
- Spot UV varnish

This book project was the combination of a collaboration between Sune Ehlers and Jon Burgerman. They wanted the book to be enjoyed on its own merits and to act as a promotional item. The book was printed in China on 600gsm grayboard coated with 128gsm art paper that was then matte laminated. A gold foil detail was added to the lid and base, and a spot UV varnish was also used on the artwork.

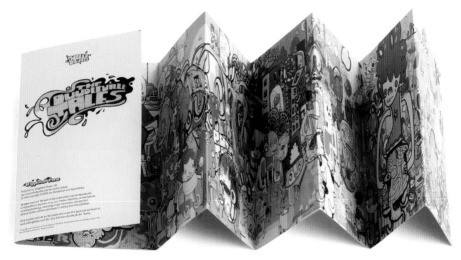

RUCKLEY CARRIER BAGS

DESIGN/CLIENT
RUCKLEY

SPECIFICATIONS
- Single-color printing
- Spot UV varnish
- Heavyweight stock

Ruckley carrier bags are made from a distinctive heavyweight board printed in single-color black prior to matte lamination and spot UV varnishing. The choice of board, and the addition of laminate, makes the bag uncommonly rigid and sturdy. These materials say that the bag is integral to the product, will not be disposed of lightly, and is an item of value in its own right. Add the subtle and sophisticated UV varnish that highlights the namestyle, plus the black rope handle, and there is no doubt that this bag and its contents will be perceived as high-quality and luxurious.

UV varnish, precisely registered over the namestyle, contrasts dramatically with the black matte surface of the bag. It is particularly effective because the rigidity of the card keeps the surface of the bag completely flat.

THERESA KATHRYN HANGTAGS

DESIGN
IE DESIGN + COMMUNICATIONS

CLIENT
THERESA KATHRYN

SPECIFICATIONS
- Two-color lithography
- Lamination
- Die-cutting
- Saddle stitching

"We wanted to bring the story of Theresa Kathryn, the person, to life by telling her inspiring story in the hangtag," says Kenny Goldstein of IE Design + Communications. This hangtag is indeed a beautifully crafted miniature book. The cover is litho-printed onto a heavyweight card, in pale blue on the outside and orange on the inside, matte laminated on both sides, intricately die-cut, creased and folded asymmetrically, saddle-stitched, and clasped with a die-cut flap. On releasing the closure, eight pages of two-color text on matte-laminated white stock are revealed to complete this exquisite hangtag. This not only extols in words the smart, successful character of Theresa Kathryn products, but also demonstrates it through the pure quality and sophistication of the tag.

235

LANDCOVE AYR

DESIGN	CLIENT
STAND	**LANDCOVE AYR**

SPECIFICATIONS
- Think from Howard Smith stock
- CMYK litho
- Extra spot varnish
- Allover spot UV

Stand designed a brochure to promote a new property development in the west end of Glasgow, Scotland. A unique selling point of the apartments was the inclusion of a selection of highly decorative wallpapers from Scottish interior designers Timorous Beasties. The screen printed patterns became the main features throughout the brochure and also inspired the illustration style. The brochure was printed on Think from Howard Smith using conventional CMYK litho with extra spot varnish.

Allover UVs are applied in the same manner as standard spot UVs, but cover a far greater area. They require careful attention at the printing stage to ensure that the UV is applied flat, does not bubble, and is dry before folding and finishing.

THIRD EYE DESIGN BOOK

DESIGN/CLIENT
THIRD EYE DESIGN

SPECIFICATIONS
➔ Cloth jacket
➔ Debossed

US promotes the work of Glasgow/New York agency Third Eye Design. Featuring nine case studies that emphasize "design effectiveness," the work in the book is visible across a vast range of industries from finance to fashion and from architecture to the arts.

The cover was made of fabric stretched over board, which was debossed with the title letters "US."

This cover has a high-quality red cloth bonded to a solid card. This gives the book the flexibility of a paperback combined with the strength of a casebound volume. The finished surface is also very receptive to embossing.

ALTA PAMPA IDENTITY AND STATIONERY

DESIGN	CLIENT
EMMI SALONEN	**ALTA PAMPA**

SPECIFICATIONS
- GF Smith Colorplan China White
- Mixed sources FSC
- 100 percent ECF virgin fiber

The creation of a corporate identity for importers of Latin American art and design for interiors preceded the design of this range of stationery. It was essential that the handmade and hand-finished qualities of these imported products could be evoked in both the corporate identity and printed material, while also appealing to high-end markets in a number of western countries. This was achieved by creating an intimate and uncomplicated motif that symbolized the intricacy of craft products and also mirrored the patterns that appear in traditional fabrics.

When used collectively, the logo motifs are suggestive of a western interior space in plan and thereby reflect the core business. This pattern appears in print on the hanging tags, but has been debossed into the surface of the paper on the corporate stationery. Debossing not only removes the need for printing, it also creates a textural and three-dimensional quality that print cannot achieve. The choice of paper stock was an important design decision and reflects the client's desire for a "high-end" appearance.

239

SUSTAINABLE BUSINESS CARDS

DESIGN/CLIENT
SIMON WINTER

SPECIFICATIONS
➔ Debossing on various recycled card and paper

These debossed business cards represent an ingenious and appropriate way of reusing waste by employing a simple method of imprinting text on previously printed material. Because these products only require a limited amount of material, they can use an almost infinite range of paper stocks, printed surfaces, and finishes. Also, the process produces a bespoke design that befits the nature of the product and heightens its sense of individuality. Requiring only manpower, the manufacturing process uses no other forms of energy and, since embossing is the means by which information is applied to the surface, there are no inks required either. The result is an inimitable and completely environmentally friendly product.

241

The lid and base of this design have been treated with a "soft-touch" finish, which gives a unique tactile quality that distinguishes the product from other potential competitors, and replaces the need for over-print lamination using varnishes derived from petrochemicals.

242

STRAWBERRY & CREAM BITES PACKAGING

DESIGN
CHESAPEAKE CORPORATION

CLIENT
FILTHY FOOD COMPANY

SPECIFICATIONS
➲ Water-based soft-touch varnish

Cardboard engineering is an essential part of the designer's toolkit when it comes to designing for the environment. With constantly improving systems of collection and recycling, increasingly supportive legislation, and better qualities of recycled material, the environmental footprint of fiberboard is reducing all the time and offers almost unbounded scope for innovation in the packaging sector.

This design represents one such example that successfully matches the aesthetic and functional properties associated with more costly materials, such as metal, yet—through its exceptional structural properties—is manufactured in the relatively lightweight and easily recycled fiberboard.

The robust construction of this design makes it a viable alternative to tin, which might otherwise have been used to package this type of high-value product. Although tin can be recycled, the overall environmental footprint of metals throughout their life cycle is greater than that of fiberboard, which can be processed, transported, and recycled with less demand on energy and resources. Given the name "springbox," the base has been designed so that it is very easy to assemble by hand and, when removed from the lid, opens out to function as a serving dish for the products within.

AIGA INVITATION

DESIGN
DESIGN ARMY

CLIENT
**AMERICAN INSTITUTE
OF GRAPHIC ARTS**

SPECIFICATIONS
- CMYK plus single spot color
- Spot varnish
- 80gsm Mohawk Superfine stock
- Die-cut

This invitation by Design Army for the American Institute of Graphic Arts' (AIGA) annual 50 Books/50 Covers awards looks to the little things in life that unexpectedly inspire. It was printed CMYK plus a single spot color and spot varnish on an A1 (594 × 841mm/23½ × 33in) sheet of 80gsm Mohawk Superfine. The intricate die-cut invitation folds down in a clockwise fashion to an undersize A4 (210 × 297mm/8¼ × 11¾in) booklet.

243

GLOSSARY

MATERIALS

Bible paper
A very thin paper, usually 40–60gsm, used for (among other things) bibles, directories, and dictionaries.

Bookbinding board
A dense fibreboard used for the covers of casebound books.

Cast-coated
Paper that has a very high-quality, high-gloss surface on one side, while the reverse remains matte and uncoated.

Coated stock
A smooth, hard-surfaced paper good for reproducing halftone images. It is created by coating the surface with china clay.

Corrugated board
Highly ridged board made up of layers of flat and corrugated paper for excellent strength and rigidity.

Kraft paper
Strong paper made from unbleached wood pulp. This material is often used for paper bags and wrapping paper due to its strength.

Laid paper
Uncoated paper with a pattern of horizontal stripes that form a slight surface texture.

Polypropylene
A flexible plastic sheet available in many different colors, including clear and frosted.

Uncoated stock
Paper that has a rougher surface than coated paper, and which is both bulkier and more opaque.

Vinyl labelling
Plastic adhesive material, available in many colors.

PRINTING

Bit-map
A generic style of computer-originated typefaces, constructed pixel by pixel. The term is also used to describe the pixilation of a digital image.

Bleed
The term used to refer to an element printed beyond the trimmed edge of the page, allowing the image, rule, or type to extend to the very edge of the printed page.

Duotone
Where two colors are printed together to make an image richer and denser in color.

Flexography
Method of printing on a web press using rubber or plastic plates with raised image and text.

Full color
Almost all mass-produced print uses lithographic inks. As a rule, full-color printing is achieved through the selective combination of four process colors: cyan, magenta, yellow, and black/key (CMYK).

Full-color black
Black created by combining cyan, magenta, and yellow inks.

Halftone
A process used to reproduce an illustration, which involves breaking it up into small dots of different densities to simulate a full tonal range.

Inkjet printing
A type of color printing that uses cyan, magenta, yellow, and black ink that is sprayed through small nozzles onto the page. Available across the entire price spectrum

for home use, as well as on commercial machines that create the highest-quality color print attainable.

Laser printing
When images are transferred to paper using laser technology. Toner particles in black or color mark the page and printing takes place directly from artwork without the need for platemaking. This is frequently the most economical form of printing for short runs.

Letterpress
A traditional method of printing, using a series of metal stamps with individual letters cast into the surface. The letters are set into a form, inked up, and pressed onto the paper's surface. The printed sheet becomes more tactile than that produced by conventional offset lithographic printing, because the type becomes debossed into the surface.

Offset lithography
Method of printing using plates with image areas attracting ink and nonimage areas repelling ink. Nonimage areas may be coated with water to repel the oily ink, or may have a surface, such as silicone, that repels ink.

PANTONE Matching System
An international professional color-matching system, which includes colors created out of the four-color set, special individual colors, metallics, fluorescents, and pastels.

PANTONE special
A specific color recipe created by Pantone, Inc. and described by a name or number.

RGB
Red, Green, Blue. The three primary colors used on screen to generate a full spectrum of color.

Screen printing
A printing method that applies ink onto the surface of the material with a squeegee through a fine silk mesh. This achieves a much denser application of ink that lithography and may be used on an almost limitless variety of surfaces.

Silkscreen printing
A printing method that applies ink onto the surface of the material through a fine silk mesh. This achieves a much denser application of ink than lithography and may be used on an almost limitless variety of surfaces.

Soy-based inks
Inks derived from soy bean oil as opposed to petroleum, and mixed with pigments, resins, and waxes. One of many different vegetable-based inks (see also vegetable-based inks).

Spot color
A special color not generated by the four-color process.

Spot varnish
See UV varnish.

Tiling
Printing a page layout in sections with overlapping edges so that the pieces can be pasted together.

Tritone
Where three colors are printed together to make an image richer and denser in color.

Two passes of ink
Printing the same color twice, with the second pass of the press printing directly over the first, to create a deeper, more intense result.

Vegetable-based inks
Inks that are made with vegetable-based oils (as opposed to mineral-based, such as petroleum) and that, as a result, are more environmentally friendly.

Web-fed press
Printing press that prints onto a continuous roll of paper. Printing is fast and can be applied to both sides of the paper at once.

FOLDING

Concertina fold
Pages folded in a zigzag manner, like the bellows of a concertina.

Cross-fold
Where a printed page is folded, then turned over and folded in the opposite direction to give multiple folds similar to those of a map.

GLOSSARY

French-fold
The method of folding
a page in half and binding
the open edges.

Gatefold
Folding where the outer edges
fold inward to meet the gutter,
creating an eight-page effect.
Often used on center-page
spreads to create impact.

Perforated fold
Printed sheets are perforated
prior to folding the sheets
down to the final page size.
This allows the French-fold
pages to be torn open easily.

Roll fold
A process whereby a long
sheet of paper is folded into
panels or pages started from
the far right, with each
subsequent panel folded back
towards the left—effectively
it is rolled back around itself.

Scoring
Required on heavier paper
(200gsm and above) to allow
folding to work properly.
On thicker card scoring is
required, otherwise the
edges can crack badly.

Throw-outs
Where the page size of
a document is bigger than its
finished size, but folded in

on itself to fit within the
document. This allows for
bigger pages than those
of standard sizes.

BINDING

Bellyband
A strip of paper or other
material that wraps around
the center of the book to
prevent the pages from
opening.

Binding screws
Small brass thumb-screws
consisting of a male and
female part, and used to bind
loose sheets together. They are
generally available in brass or
nickel-plated (silver).

Binding tape
Tape or other material that
binds around the spine of
a book to protect the edges
and allow for easy opening.

Burstbound
The pages of the document
are gathered but not sewn. The
folded edges are perforated
and glue is inserted, which
soaks into the perfs.

Casebound
Binding using glue to hold
sections of pages (signatures)
to a case made of thick board

bound in plastic, fabric,
or leather.

Comb binding
Similar in principle to wire
binding, a machine is used
to punch a row of small holes
along the edge of the book, a
plastic "comb" is then pushed
through the holes to create
the binding.

Flush-trimmed cover
Where a casebound book
has its cover boards trimmed
flush to the text pages,
creating a smooth,
crisp finish.

Half Canadian binding
A method similar to wire
binding, although the cover
has a spine and the wire is
bound through the back cover,
which has two additional
crease folds.

Japanese binding
Thread is bound from the back
to the front of the book around
the outside edge of the spine.
Used primarily for binding
loose sheets.

Perfect binding
Pages are glued to the cover
and held together with a strip
of adhesive, giving the spine
of the brochure a completely
flat appearance.

246

Saddle-stitching
The standard method of binding for literature; pages are secured with stitches or staples placed through the centerfold of nested signatures.

Singer-sewn binding
Sewing along the centerfold of a document using an industrial version of the household sewing machine.

Wire binding/ wire-o binding
A binding method by which a thin spiral of wire is passed through a series of prepunched holes along the edge of the pages to be bound.

FINISHING

Debossed
Having a surface pattern pressed into the page. This process is also known as blind embossing.

Die-cut
The method by which intricate shapes can be cut from the page. This process requires a custom-made die, which has a sharp steel edge constructed to cut the required shape.

Embossed
Having a raised surface pattern. This is created by using a male and female form.

Engraving
Printing method using a metal plate with an image cut into its surface that holds ink and is then pressed into the paper.

Foil blocking
A printing method that transfers a metallic foil to the page through the application of a metal block and heat.

Forme cut
A die forme is used to cut a document to a non-standard shape.

Gloss/metallic foil
Uses the same process as foil blocking, but a metallic foil is used instead with a gloss printed directly on top.

Hand finishing
Anything that cannot be produced by in-line machinery will require hand finishing. This could be anything from folding in scored pages and throw-outs to inserting added elements or binding a document together by hand.

Hot-foil stamping
Application of heat and metallic film in a speciality printing process that produces a shiny design on paper, vinyl, textiles, wood, hard plastic, leather, and other materials.

Kiss cut
Similar to die-cutting, but does not pass right the way through the sheet. Mostly used for making sticker sheets where the backing paper must remain intact.

Lamination
The application of a clear matte or gloss protective film over the printed surface of a sheet of paper.

Laser die-cut
A very precise method of cutting out elements from stock. Highly creative shapes can be successfully cut in the page, way beyond the abilities of conventional die-cutting.

Laser etching
Ssing this process, patterns or text can be written in high resolution and transferred to the underlying material via reactive ion etching.

Pigment blocking
A process similar to foil blocking, but using colored film.

Thermography
A relief effect created by dusting a special powder onto a printed image while still wet, then passing the sheet through a heating device.

UV varnish
A plastic-based varnish applied by screen printing, and available in matte, satin, and gloss finishes. It can be applied over the entire surface or treated as a spot varnish, enabling the designer to print elements purely as a varnish or to highlight selected elements on the page.

CONTACT DETAILS

Deborah Kings.

totalcontent. Studio The Abbey, Warwick Road
Southam, Warwickshire United Kingdom CV47 0HN
T +01926 812286 M +07870 751958 F +01926 811386
deb@totalcontent.co.uk www.totalcontent.co.uk

999 Design
www.999group.co.uk

Absolute Zero Degrees
www.absolutezerodegrees.co.uk

Airside
www.airside.co.uk

Alexander Isley Inc.
www.alexanderisley.com

Asa San Marino
www.gruppoasa.com

Astrid Stavro
www.astridstavro.com

Base Design
www.basedesign.com

BBDO
www.bbdo.com

Blast
www.blast.co.uk

Blok Design
www.blockdesign.com

Boxal
www.boxal.com

Catalogtree
www.catalogtree.net

Chesapeake Corporation
www.cskcorp.com

Crown Holdings, Inc.
www.crowncork.com

Crush Design
www.crushed.co.uk

Design Army
www.designarmy.com

Design Bridge
www.designbridge.com

Design N/A
www.design-na.co.uk

Dotzero Design
www.dotzerodesign.com

Dragon
www.dragonrouge.co.uk

Earth Greetings
www.earthgreetings.com.au

Ecojot
www.ecojot.com

Emmi Salonen
www.emmi.co.uk

Flipflop Design Ltd.
www.flipflopdesign.co.uk

The Formation Creative Consultants
www.theformation-cc.co.uk

Four IV
www.fouriv.com

Fuelhaus
www.fuelhaus.com

Giulio Turturro
www.giulioturturro.com

Glud & Marstrand
www.glud-marstrand.com

Greg Barber Co.
www.gregbarberco.com

Hat-Trick Design
www.hat-trickdesign.co.uk

Hello Duudle
www.duudle.dk

Helvetica
www.jkr.co.uk

Iamalwayshungry
www.iamalwayshungry.com

IE Design + Communications
www.iedesign.com

Inaria
www. inaria-design.com

Inksurge
www.inksurge.com

Iwantdesign
www.iwantdesign.co.uk

Joliat
www.joliat.net

KBDA
www.kbda.com

Kendall Ross Brand Development and Design
www.kendallross.com

Kukusi
www.kukusi.com

Laura Varsky
www.lauravarsky.com.ar

Little Otsu
www.littleotsu.com

Loewy
www.loewygroup.com

MadeThought
www.madethought.com

Main Studio
www.mainstudio.com

Matt Graif Design
www.mattgraif.com

CONTACT DETAILS

The Military
www.thmilitary.co.uk

Mode
www.mode-online.co.uk

Modern Dog
www.moderndog.com

MSLK
www.mslk.com

NB: Studio
www.nbstudio.co.uk

Nevis Design Consultants
www.nevisdesign.co.uk

Nick Clark
www.nickclarkdesign.co.uk

Oiko
www.oiko.com.au

Oliver Walker
www.onstudio.co.uk

Olli & Lime
www.olliandlime.com

OrangeYouGlad
www.orangeyouglad.com

Palazzolo Design
www.palazzolodesign.com

Paprika
www.paprika.com

Paul Cartwright Branding
www.paulcartwrightbranding.co.uk

Peekaboo Design
www.peekaboodesign.co.uk

PH.D
www.phdla.com

Pixel Organics
www.pixelorganics.com

Prank Design
www.prankdesign.com

Radford Wallis
www.radfordwallis.com

Raidy Printing Group
www.raidy.com

Red Design
www.red-design.co.uk

Rinzen
www.rinzen.com

Ruckley
www.ruckley.com

Saturday
www.saturday-london.com

SEA Design
www.seadesign.co.uk

Sheaff Dorman Purins
www.sheaff.com

Simon Winter
www.simonwinterdesign.co.uk

The Small Stakes
www.thesmallstakes.com

Spin
www.spin.co.uk

Stand
www.stand-united.co.uk

Standard13
www.standard13.com

Steven Wilson
www.breedlondon.com

Studio Locaso
www.studiolocaso.com.au

Studio Output
www.studio-output.com

Subplot Design Inc.
www.subplot.com

Superbacana Design
www.superbacanadesign.com.br

Surface/Miwa Yanagi
www.yanagimiwa.net

Third Eye Design
www.thirdeyedesign.co.uk

Turnstyle
www.turnstylestudio.com

Vault49
www.vault49.com

Voice
www.voicedesign.net

Vrontikis Design Office
www.35k.com

Wunderburg Design
www.wunderburg-design.de

Zion Graphics
www.ziongraphics.com

Zip Design
www.zipdesign.co.uk

INDEX

INDEX

255

ABOUT THE AUTHORS

Edward Denison writes regularly about subjects across a wide range of design disciplines, and has received critical acclaim for his written and photographic work through numerous printed and broadcast media internationally.

Roger Fawcett-Tang is founder and creative director of Struktur Design, which has developed a reputation for clean understated typography, attention to detail, and logical organization of information and imagery. It has won various design awards, and has been featured in numerous design books and international magazines.

Jessica Glaser and Carolyn Knight are partners in the UK design firm Bright Pink, which serves clients in industries including textiles, health care, finance, and nonprofit organizations. Both are senior lecturers in Graphic Communications within the University of Wolverhampton School of Art and Design. They are the authors of *Diagrams* and *The Graphic Design Exercise Book*, both published by RotoVision.

Established in 1929, Loewy was the world's first design agency. Founder Raymond Loewy is something of a design legend. His many iconic works include the Coca-Cola bottle; identities for Shell, Exxon, and McLaren; The Greyhound bus, bullet train, and Studebaker car; and interiors for Concorde and Skylab. Today Loewy is a full-service marketing and communications agency that offers a broad range of core services, with expertise in disciplines as diverse as corporate identity, branding, brochures, advertising, web sites, catalogs, packaging, sales promotion, and direct marketing.

A designer with more than 18 years of agency experience, Scott Witham graduated in 1992 from Duncan of Jordanstone College of Art, Scotland, with an Honors degree in graphic design and typography. Over the years he has worked for some of Scotland's best-known agencies, designing for clients including Sony, Orange, Lurpak, Virgin, and the Royal Bank of Scotland Group. He founded Traffic Design Consultants in 2002 where he continues to work as Creative Director.